2012

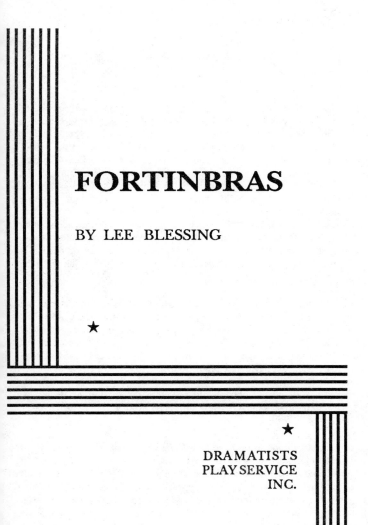

FORTINBRAS

BY LEE BLESSING

★

DRAMATISTS
PLAY SERVICE
INC.

FORTINBRAS
Copyright © 1992, Lee Blessing

All Rights Reserved

For Jeanne

FORTINBRAS received its world premiere at the La Jolla Playhouse (Des McAnuff, Artistic Director; Alan Levey, Managing Director), in La Jolla, California, on June 18, 1991. It was directed by Des McAnuff; the scene design was by Robert Brill; the costume design was by Susan Hilferty; the lighting design was by Chris Parry; the music was composed and performed by Michael Roth; the sound design was by Kenneth Ted Bible and Michael Roth, and the stage manager was Andy Tighe. The cast was as follows:

HAMLET ....Don Reilly
OSRIC ....Jefferson Mays
HORATIO ....Ralph Bruneau
ENGLISH AMBASSADOR ....William Cain
FORTINBRAS...Daniel Jenkins
CAPTAIN OF THE NORWEGIAN ARMY............Paul Gutrecht
MARCELLUS...James Crawford
BARNARDO ....James Kiernan
POLISH MAIDENS ....Archer Martin; Kim C. Walsh
POLONIUS ....William Cain
OPHELIA ....Laura Linney
CLAUDIUS ....Jonathan Freeman
GERTRUDE ....Devon Allen
LAERTES ....Josh Sebers

CHARACTERS

Living

HAMLET, Prince of Denmark
OSRIC, member of the Danish court
HORATIO, friend of Hamlet
ENGLISH AMBASSADOR
FORTINBRAS, Prince of Norway
CAPTAIN of the Norwegian Army
MARCELLUS, a sentinel
BARNARDO, a sentinel
FIRST MAIDEN
SECOND MAIDEN

Other

POLONIUS, the Court Councillor
OPHELIA, his daughter
CLAUDIUS, King of Denmark
GERTRUDE, Queen of Denmark
LAERTES, Polonius's son

PLACE

The Castle at Elsinore, Denmark.

TIME

Immediately following the events of *Hamlet*.

FORTINBRAS

ACT ONE

Scene 1

The final tableau from Hamlet. *Horatio kneels holding Hamlet, who's mortally wounded. Laertes, Gertrude and Claudius all lie dead. Osric is also present.*

HAMLET.
Oh God, Horatio, what a wounded name,
Things standing thus unknown, shall live
      behind me!
If thou didst ever hold me in thy heart,
Absent thee from felicity awhile,
And in this harsh world draw thy breath in
      pain,
To tell my story.
(A march afar off. Exit Osric.)
             What warlike noise is this?
OSRIC.   *(Reentering.)*
Young Fortinbras, with conquest come from
      Poland,
To th' ambassadors of England gives
This warlike volley.
HAMLET.
             Oh, I die, Horatio!
The potent poison quite o'ercrows my
      spirit.
I cannot live to hear the news from England,
But I do prophesy th' election lights

On Fortinbras. He has my dying voice.
So tell him, with th' occurrents, more and
          less,
Which have solicited — the rest is silence.
(Hamlet dies.)
HORATIO.
Now cracks a noble heart. Good night, sweet
          Prince,
And flights of angels sing thee to thy rest.
*(Sound of a military drum. Enter an English Ambassador. He is fol-
lowed after a moment by Fortinbras and his Norwegian Captain.)*
ENGLISH AMBASSADOR.
                    The sight is dismal;
And our affairs from England come too late.
The ears are senseless that should give us
          hearing
To tell him his commandment is fulfilled,
That Rosencrantz and Guildenstern are —
FORTINBRAS. Excuse me. *(The Ambassador stops, surprised.)*
Could you please be quiet, please? In fact, could you wait
outside? Please? *(The Ambassador hesitates. The Captain takes a
menacing step towards him. The Ambassador exits.)* I never liked
English guys. You're Horatio, right? I remember you.
HORATIO. Fortinbras?
FORTINBRAS.   Hi. So — God, what is all this?
HORATIO.   I beg of you, give order that these bodies
High on a stage be placed to the view —
FORTINBRAS.   Yeah, ok — but what happened?
HORATIO.   The people must know —
FORTINBRAS.   Well, sure ... everyone's going to know. You
can't keep something like this quiet. Captain, why don't you
take these, um — *(Indicates the bodies.)* and put them some-
place safe for now, ok? *(The Captain grabs the body of Laertes,
looks around.)* Is everyone dead? The whole family, I mean?
HORATIO.   Two families.
FORTINBRAS.   Two?! No one's left? Of the whole royal — ?
HORATIO.   No one. *(The Captain drags Laertes out.)*
FORTINBRAS.   *(Picking up Hamlet's foil.)* They all just kill

each other, or what?

HORATIO. Yes, m'lord. I was here to see everything. *(Pointing to Osric.)* He was, too. So were others, but they all seem to have ... *(He trails off as he notices everyone at court but he and Osric are gone.)*

FORTINBRAS. I don't blame them. Nobody likes being a witness. You stayed, though. That's good. What's your name?

OSRIC. Osric, m'lord.

FORTINBRAS. So what happened, Osric?

OSRIC. I don't know, m'lord.

FORTINBRAS. But he said you were here.

OSRIC. I was — I mean I am, but —

FORTINBRAS. Afraid to get involved, eh?

OSRIC. Yes, m'lord.

FORTINBRAS. Imagine how I feel. I'm on my way back from the wars against the Poles — just stopped in to say hi — and look at this. What are these foils for?

HORATIO. There was a fencing contest — Hamlet and Laertes. But it was a trap. One of the sword tips was poisoned.

FORTINBRAS. *(Who was about to touch the tip.)* Really? *(Fortinbras hands the foil to Osric. The Captain returns. The Captain drags out Gertrude's body.)* So where were we? The sword was poisoned — by who?

HORATIO. Claudius.

FORTINBRAS. The King?

HORATIO. He also poisoned the wine in that chalice. He and Laertes conspired against my lord Hamlet. The Queen was innocent, but drank the wine by mistake and —

FORTINBRAS. Hold it, hold it! I'm never going to follow all that. *(Picking up a pearl from the floor.)* What's this?

HORATIO. A pearl, m'lord. It was in the wine.

FORTINBRAS. In the wine?

OSRIC. As a prize.

FORTINBRAS. Yeah? Neat. Not much of a prize, though, if the wine's poisoned. This was Claudius's idea? *(The Captain returns, drags off Claudius's body.)*

HORATIO. If you'll let me explain —

FORTINBRAS. Say, who's in charge now, anyway?

HORATIO. M'lord?

FORTINBRAS. *(Nodding towards Hamlet's corpse.)* It's obviously none of these guys.

HORATIO. I'm not sure ...

FORTINBRAS. Nobody's left, eh? I'll tell you what we do in Norway. We find out who died last —

OSRIC. Last, my lord?

FORTINBRAS. They must've died in some order. So what was it?

HORATIO. Um ... the Queen, Laertes —

OSRIC. No, the King.

HORATIO. The King first?

OSRIC. *After* the Queen.

HORATIO. Didn't Laertes — ?

FORTINBRAS. *Who died last?*

OSRIC. Hamlet.

HORATIO. Hamlet. *(The Captain returns. He removes Hamlet's body.)*

FORTINBRAS. So — when he died, he was the king, essentially. Did he say anything about who should succeed him?

OSRIC. You, m'lord.

HORATIO. He said he *assumed* it would be you.

OSRIC. Definitely you. He said.

FORTINBRAS. You're kidding me.

HORATIO. Of course you must be chosen by the Electors.

OSRIC. A mere formality. After all, who's left? *(Horatio shoots Osric an angry look. The Captain reenters.)*

FORTINBRAS. Me? That is so hard to believe. Captain — go bring me the head of the Electors. *(The Captain exits.)* This is a real surprise. I had no idea you guys liked Norwegians this much. Of course, you don't really, do you? *(Horatio and Osric look at each other embarrassedly.)*

OSRIC. *(Kneeling.)* I for one love Norwegians.

FORTINBRAS. Yeah? Well, great. Osric — you look like a pretty bright guy. *(Horatio gives an incredulous laugh. Fortinbras gives Osric the pearl.)* Take this. I want you to gather up everything here: foils, chalices, pearls — everything, and give it all a good wash.

HORATIO. M'lord — !

FORTINBRAS. Wash the floor, too. Get rid of any ... wine stains.

HORATIO. M'lord, we need the proof —

FORTINBRAS. We have proof.

HORATIO. The bodies, you mean?

FORTINBRAS. No — you can get bodies anyplace. We've got much better proof than that. We've got testimony.

HORATIO. Testimony?

FORTINBRAS. Yeah. You. Osric. Testimony. Now, look — while Osric's cleaning up in here, I want you to go back to whatever room you're in and write down everything that happened here. I want a full report, ok? That's the only way I'm going to figure it out. Then maybe I can start to make up the truth.

HORATIO. Make up?

FORTINBRAS. That's a poor choice of words. What I mean is nothing's true until it's certified — right? You're in government, sort of. You know that. And nothing gets certified, except by the proper authorities. And I'm the proper authorities now. Right? *(With a look at Osric.)* I mean, right? *(Fortinbras smiles cheerfully. Lights fade to black.)*

Scene 2

The battlements of Elsinore. Fortinbras stands looking through a telescope. Osric is nearby, with Marcellus and Barnardo. They hold up a large tapestry for inspection. On the other side of Fortinbras, Horatio stands holding a parchment.

OSRIC. *(As Fortinbras continues to scan the horizon.)* It used to hang in the Queen's chamber. She had it moved after the unfortunate —

FORTINBRAS. Sure. I can understand that. *(With a quick glance at it.)* Looks pretty good, though.

OSRIC. It is. Just this little ... rip here, you see, and —

FORTINBRAS.   No blood on the front of it?

OSRIC.   No, all on the back. A little sewing, and —

FORTINBRAS.   Great. I like it. Put it in my rooms.

OSRIC.   Which will be?

FORTINBRAS.   The King's chambers. *(Osric nods.)*

HORATIO.   You haven't been elected yet, m'lord.

FORTINBRAS.   Ok. Just put it outside the King's chambers for now. What else is there?

OSRIC.   *(Searching through a pile of regal objects with Marcellus and Barnardo.)* Let me see ...

FORTINBRAS.   *(Looking through the telescope again.)* Where were we, Horatio?

HORATIO.   My lord Hamlet's ship had just been set upon by ... pirates.

FORTINBRAS.   Pirates? Get out of here.

HORATIO.   It happened, m'lord.

FORTINBRAS.   Did you see these pirates?

HORATIO.   No, m'lord.

FORTINBRAS.   Right. Go on.

HORATIO.   *(Reading from the parchment.)* "The pirates, on learning Prince Hamlet's identity, immediately released him — "

FORTINBRAS.   Released him? Why?

HORATIO.   He promised to do them a favor ... sometime. *(Fortinbras looks incredulous.)* It happened, m'lord.

FORTINBRAS.   Go on.

HORATIO.   "Hamlet then sent for me — "

OSRIC.   *(Holding up a bouquet of dried flowers.)* Dead flowers, m'lord.

FORTINBRAS.   Dead flowers?

OSRIC.   They were Lady Ophelia's — from her unfortunate period. After she died, the Queen kept them.

FORTINBRAS.   *(Finding this morbid.)* Oh. Keep them anyway. Put them on the wall or something.

HORATIO.   May I continue?

FORTINBRAS.   I wish you wouldn't, Horatio. This was all pretty unbelievable when I read it last night. I thought maybe if you read it to me yourself, but —

HORATIO.   It's what happened.

FORTINBRAS.   I can't help that.

HORATIO.   I was in a unique position to *know*.

FORTINBRAS.   So what? I mean, who can understand all this stuff? A ghost appears to Hamlet and tells him his uncle killed his father, so Hamlet pretends to go crazy — or maybe he really does, who cares? — and he decides to kill his uncle. But he stalls around for a long time instead, kills a guy who's *not* his uncle, gets sent to England, gets rescued by pirates, comes back and kills everybody — including himself. I mean, come *on*.

HORATIO.   *(As the others hold up a small, wooden prayer bench.)* The King's prayer bench, m'lord. It's hardly been used.

FORTINBRAS.   Yeah, great — for my chambers. *(To Horatio, with disbelief.)* You really saw a ghost?

HORATIO.   Yes. Old King Hamlet.

FORTINBRAS.   And Hamlet saw this ghost?

HORATIO.   And Marcellus, and Barnardo.

FORTINBRAS.   *(To them.)* You did?

MARCELLUS.   We think we did.

BARNARDO.   It was dark.

HORATIO.   They stood here with me, on this very battlement, and saw Hamlet's father's ghost.

FORTINBRAS.   My father's dead; I've never seen *his* ghost.

HORATIO.   Your father was killed in fair and equal combat.

FORTINBRAS.   My father was killed, as you well know, by Hamlet's father. Old Hamlet killed Old Fortinbras — in a duel, of all things — on the day Hamlet was born. I was just an infant myself. Made me kind of an orphan.

HORATIO.   Forgive me, lord. I merely —

FORTINBRAS.   And because my father was an even worse gambler than he was a swordsman, he'd agreed to give certain lands to Denmark if he lost. *(Looking though the telescope.)* Those lands, over there. My father's ghost doesn't come back because he'd be ashamed to face me. Wish he could, though. It'd be nice to see what he looked like. For once. *(A beat.)* Well, they'll be my lands again soon enough, providing my captain ever brings me the *head of the Electors!* Osric, why is he having so much trouble?

13

OSRIC. The Electors are ... a bit reluctant about coming to see you, m'lord.

FORTINBRAS. Why?

OSRIC. The phrase you've been using, "Bring me the *head* of the Electors." It seems to make them nervous.

FORTINBRAS. You're kidding. Oh, God. I'm so sorry — that's really funny. I never heard it that way till right now. No wonder they don't want to come. *(The Captain enters and bows. He has a sealed parchment and a cloth bag, weighted down by something the shape and heft of a human head. He hands Fortinbras the parchment. Fortinbras reads it.)* Good. Good, good, good. I've been elected. *(To Osric.)* Take all these things and put them in the King's chambers. We'll go through them later.

OSRIC. Yes, m'lor — *(Correcting himself, with a deep bow.)* Yes, my *sovereign* lord. And may I be the first to say —

FORTINBRAS. *(Taking the sack from the Captain.)* Is this for me, too? *(Osric, Marcellus and Barnardo instantly bundle up everything.)* What were you saying, Osric?

OSRIC. It'll keep. *(Osric, Marcellus and Barnardo hurry out with the objects.)*

FORTINBRAS. Horatio, we've got to have a new story.

HORATIO. But there's only the truth.

FORTINBRAS. That's the problem. You want to tell everyone in Denmark that their entire royal family killed itself, plus a family of reasonably innocent nobles, *plus* two attendant lords? Good God, Horatio — how much do you think people can take? No one wants to hear their whole royal family's incompetent. Personally, I think we should just replace the whole story.

HORATIO. Replace it?

FORTINBRAS. We need a story that'll do something for us: explain the bodies, preserve the monarchy, give the people some kind of focus for all their — I don't know — anger, loss, what*ever*. And most of all, something that'll show people that everything that's happened up till now had to happen so that I could become king. I know how I'd like to explain it.

HORATIO. How?

FORTINBRAS. A Polish spy.

14

HORATIO. A Polish — ?!

FORTINBRAS. Exactly! It's the perfect idea. Look — the Poles, bitter at Claudius's pact with my uncle to grant me and my troops free passage through Denmark so that I can kick their Polish butts, send a spy to the court here in Elsinore. His job is to destroy the entire Danish royal family. You know, as a lesson to all who would conspire against the Polish crown — all that crap. Anyhow, he successfully sabotages the fencing match, bares the swordtip, poisons the weapon, the wine — see how easy this is, all one guy — sets the unsuspecting participants against each other in a sort of frenzy of sudden rage and paranoia, and executes the most extraordinary mass-regicide in the history of Europe.

HORATIO. But —

FORTINBRAS. *And* we can even add a lot of stuff about the horror when the royal Danes, each mortally wounded and/or poisoned, suddenly realized that Poland had achieved its ultimate revenge — blah, blah, blah.

HORATIO. That's not what happened.

FORTINBRAS. I bet it will be. It's just so much better. Anyone can understand it. And the best thing is, it gives me that historical reason-for-being that's so important to a new king. You see? I'm here to save Denmark from an imminent attack by Poland. *(Horatio looks incredibly dubious.)* Of course, if you want to tell people that ridiculous story of yours, be my guest. But I'll bet mine's the one that catches on. In fact, Captain, I want you to promulgate the true story you've just heard.

CAPTAIN. Which true story?

FORTINBRAS. The Polish —

CAPTAIN. Yes, my liege.

FORTINBRAS. Make it known throughout Denmark. And begin the amalgamation of Danish and Norwegian forces, preparatory to a full invasion.

CAPTAIN. Of — ?

FORTINBRAS. *Po*land.

CAPTAIN. Yes, my liege.

HORATIO. Invasion — !?

FORTINBRAS. Relax. If people believe your story we won't invade anywhere. Then again, if they believe my story — well — I'll *have* to invade Poland. *(Sighs.)* And of course I'll have to find a Polish spy.
HORATIO. But there is none!
FORTINBRAS. That'll make it harder. But maybe we don't even need to catch him. Maybe just looking's the best. This story's going to work out great. Get going, Captain. *(The Captain exits.)*
HORATIO. Sire, what you're suggesting is infamous.
FORTINBRAS. What? The invasion? That won't really happen. We'll just march the army to the Polish border, rattle the old swords for twenty minutes and come home. Nobody'll get hurt, and I'll prove to you that I'm right about this story thing and you're not. Hey — want to know what's in the sack?
HORATIO. No, sire —
FORTINBRAS. Come on — take a look. Closer. *Closer!* *(Horatio steps closer.)* What could it be, I wonder? My captain brings me a lot of stuff. He's ambitious. *(Fortinbras peers into the bag.)* Ooo — man! You want to see?
HORATIO. No — ! *(Fortinbras pulls a melon out of the bag.)*
FORTINBRAS. Is that a beauty? *(Horatio can't help but give a sigh of profound relief.)* I wondered what I was going to have for lunch. You got a knife? *(Horatio hands him a knife. Fortinbras slices the melon.)* That was a weird sigh, Horatio. What'd you think I had in here, the head of the Electors? *(Fortinbras laughs.)* You thought it was a head. Instead, it's going to feed us both. There's a lesson in that. *(Offering Horatio a slice.)* Eat it. *(Horatio starts to eat.)* You know, this is a lucky place, Elsinore.
HORATIO. Lucky?
FORTINBRAS. For me it is. How many people walk through the door and — boom, they're king? That's lucky. *(A beat.)* So what was Hamlet like, anyway?
HORATIO. Sire?
FORTINBRAS. He was complex or something, right? *(Horatio nods.)* Sorry he's gone. I was always going to talk to him. You know, about ... various matters. You went to Wittenberg

16

with him?

HORATIO.   I did.

FORTINBRAS.   I wanted to go to college. My uncle wouldn't let me, though. Afraid I'd get too powerful. Hamlet read a lot, didn't he? Words, I mean?

HORATIO.   Yes, sire.

FORTINBRAS.   Good times at Wittenberg, eh? Yeah, college life.

HORATIO.   I could ... teach you.

FORTINBRAS.   Teach me?

HORATIO.   Tutor you. Give you the benefit of my years there.

FORTINBRAS.   You want to do that for me? How come?

HORATIO.   Every prince needs an education.

FORTINBRAS.   Right now I know how to win battles. What else is there?

HORATIO.   Diplomacy —

FORTINBRAS.   That's just battles without soldiers. I do that great.

HORATIO.   Ethics.

FORTINBRAS.   Oops. We're back to telling the truth again.

HORATIO.   My lord Hamlet's life requires the truth —

FORTINBRAS.   It's just a vicious circle with you, isn't it? Try to understand this, ok? I'm not here to finish their story. They were all here to begin mine. *(Hefting the remainder of the melon in his hand, giving it to Horatio.)* It's the new perspective. Master it.

HORATIO.   Yes, my liege. *(Horatio bows, exits with the melon. Fortinbras turns and stares through the telescope at the horizon. After a moment, the ghost of Polonius enters. Fortinbras doesn't notice him. Polonius carefully reaches out to touch the telescope and startles Fortinbras.)*

FORTINBRAS.   Jesus! You scared me. Who are you? *(Polonius smiles anxiously. Fortinbras looks closer.)* Do I know you? *(Polonius nods.)* Polonius? *(Polonius nods.)* But you're — *(Polonius gives an gentle shrug, reaches out for the telescope.)* What do you want? This? *(Fortinbras gives it to Polonius, who seems pleased to hold it. Polonius stares through it this way and that.)* Don't you get much of a view where you are? *(Polonius pays no attention.)* My new lands? Is that what you're looking at? *(Polonius, still looking through the telescope, nods.)* Is there something you want to tell me? Something I should know? *(Polonius nods.)* What is it? *(Polonius starts to answer, but somehow can't bring himself to speak. He waves his hand dismissively, as though it's not really worth saying.)* Is it complex? *(Polonius turns, hands Fortinbras the telescope and nods. Polonius exits. Fortinbras stares after him. Lights fade to black.)*

Scene 3

The castle. Horatio and Osric collide as they cross paths in a hurry. Osric holds some objects, including the foils from Scene 1. Some of these spill to the floor.

HORATIO.   Watch it!

OSRIC.   Oh — !

HORATIO.   Idiot. What's wrong with you?

OSRIC.   Nothing's wrong with me. *I'm* well-adjusted. *(Dropping another foil.)* Damn!

HORATIO.   Where are you taking these?

OSRIC.   The King's chambers. Fortin — *King* Fortinbras wants them for the wall.

HORATIO.   Those are from the duel!

OSRIC.   They've been washed.

HORATIO.   You're not taking them. *(Horatio takes the foils from him.)*

OSRIC.   Horatio — !

HORATIO.   *This is the sword that killed your Prince!* *(Looking at the other foil.)* Or this is!

OSRIC.   They're not swords anymore. They're decor. Now give them back. *(Horatio sighs, returns them.)*

HORATIO.   He says no one will believe us.

OSRIC.   Believe us what?

HORATIO.   When we tell what really happened.

OSRIC.   Why would we do that?

HORATIO. For the sake of the truth!

OSRIC. Horatio, get a grip on yourself. Monarchs change and we change with them. It's natural as the wind and rain. Do you want *your* head to end up in a sack?

HORATIO. That wasn't a head; it was a melon. I saw it. I ate it.

OSRIC. Then ... what happened to the Electors?

HORATIO. They're probably running for the countryside.

OSRIC. They were always nervous. I wouldn't be surprised if one of them was the Polish spy who — *(Horatio grabs Osric by the collar.)*

HORATIO. *There is no Polish spy!*

OSRIC. I know, I know!! But if there were one —

HORATIO. *There's none!*

OSRIC. But if there were — you're choking me — if there were — and we know there's not — one of the Electors might actually be — *(Horatio throws him to the floor in disgust.)*

HORATIO. You're a fool.

OSRIC. *(Getting his breath.)* Thank you, Horatio.

HORATIO. So is Fortinbras. He's an absolute child. He makes Laertes look cultured.

OSRIC. I like him. *(Horatio gives Osric a look.)* Well, he's cheerful. It's not like Hamlet — wandering around, looking morose all the time, wearing earth tones. Fortinbras does things. He gives orders we can follow. So what if he lies a little? Claudius lied a lot. Honestly, Horatio, I think you should just try to get on board for once.

HORATIO. And that's as deeply as you want to examine things?

OSRIC. Goodness, yes. I wouldn't examine them that deeply if I could avoid it. Oh, I know — they say the unexamined life is not worth living. But the examined life is also not worth living, and it's a great deal more painful. I'd've thought Prince Hamlet's experience would have shown you that. *(Osric starts to leave again.)*

HORATIO. I'm going to tell the truth! To everyone I meet.

OSRIC. I'll warn them. *(Osric exits. Lights fade to black.)*

Scene 4

Fortinbras in the King's chambers. His royal bed is imposing. The tapestry from Scene 2 now hangs on the wall. Likewise, Claudius's prayer bench, Ophelia's dead flowers and the foils from the duel have been worked into the decor. Fortinbras, dressed for lounging, sits on the foot of the bed, talking with the Captain and toying with the crown.

FORTINBRAS.   So, when'll they be ready to march?

CAPTAIN.   In the morning, sire.

FORTINBRAS.   Great. Tell my generals to go right up to Poland and stop, ok? This is not a real invasion or anything — just some dancing around.

CAPTAIN.   Very good, sire. *(The Captain exits. Horatio enters.)*

FORTINBRAS.   Horatio — good! Come on in. How about this room, eh? Finally got it the way I like it. So tell me, what'd they do with those guys at the funeral today? The ones that got unruly.

HORATIO.   They were chastened and sent home.

FORTINBRAS.   That Hamlet was a popular guy. Four graves, and everybody's jumping into his. Hope a lot of people will jump on my grave when I'm dead.

HORATIO.   I'm sure they will, sire.

FORTINBRAS.   You're funny, Horatio. I should like that more than I do.

HORATIO.   About the issue of sacred ground.

FORTINBRAS.   Sorry — they all get sacred ground. End of argument.

HORATIO.   But Claudius? He killed his brother.

FORTINBRAS.   So you say.

HORATIO.   He slept with his brother's wife.

FORTINBRAS.   Hey — he married her.

HORATIO.   *And* he killed her.

FORTINBRAS.   An accident.

HORATIO.   A murder plot gone awry is not an accident. He

usurped the throne from its rightful heir —

FORTINBRAS. He was elected, same as me.

HORATIO. Precisely.

FORTINBRAS. He has to be buried in sacred ground, or the Polish spy story doesn't work. I wish you'd get a sense of priorities. Come here and sit down. Come on, come on — sit. *(Horatio sits uncomfortably next to Fortinbras on the bed.)* How you doing on that story of yours? Anybody believe you yet?

HORATIO. One or two have ... come close.

FORTINBRAS. It's not easy, I know. I used to tell the truth all the time. People would get incredibly disappointed. I'd say, "But that's what really happened." *(Sighs.)* I was so unpopular. Then I thought, "Wait a minute — I'm a prince. And some-day, a king." And it's far more important for a king to be popular than to recount a bunch of random events the way they actually happened. You see what I'm saying? If the truth distances me from my people, then how can it be the truth? *(A beat.)* You know what I saw through my telescope? Up on the battlements?

HORATIO. No, sire.

FORTINBRAS. I saw the future. I saw a lot of farmers, cows, trees — but I also saw the future. And the future, Horatio, is that this kingdom gets more and more powerful.

HORATIO. How?

FORTINBRAS. First we get the army back from Poland, once we've made the spy story look good. Then we take it up to Norway and break off a few of my uncle's legs. Then, we turn around to the rest of Europe and say — and this is the great part, we only have to *say* it — "Watch out for Denway."

HORATIO. Denway?

FORTINBRAS. Or Normark — it doesn't matter. The point is, the combined power of our two countries will be over-whelming. Horatio, we are on the brink of the great Norween-ish age of Europe!

HORATIO. Norween — ?

FORTINBRAS. Or Daneweegian — it doesn't matter.

HORATIO. Sire —

FORTINBRAS. Think of it! Anywhere a Daneweegian goes,

he'll be safe. With military power like this, we can sit and polish our weapons till the end of time.

HORATIO. I gave my oath to Hamlet —

FORTINBRAS. Hamlet's dead now. I'm your King. You have wonderful loyalty, Horatio. You just have to learn how to point it in different directions. Think of it! For the first time in your life you could be proud to be Norweenish!

HORATIO. No! No, sire — strike off my head if you must, but do not ask me to renounce my oath. An oath is larger than a kingship, and a kingship is larger, may I say, than you! You can never tempt me with petty conquests!

FORTINBRAS. Petty? It's all of Norway.

HORATIO. A kingdom is not a plaything, and we are not boys! A king rules to serve his people, not himself. If you learn nothing from the tragic reign of Claudius, learn that.

FORTINBRAS. Hey, hey, hey! No need to get rigid about this. I just wanted to get you in on the ground-floor of the myth thing. The reign of Fortinbras needs one small, tidy conquest. Then we can relax and nourish our new nation on the very myth we've created. That's how a real leader leads. And it's how a leader's friend is his friend. I could use a friend, Horatio. Not like Osric. Someone ... like Hamlet had.

HORATIO. Hamlet earned his friends.

FORTINBRAS. That's fine, if you've got the time. But if you're going places like me, friendships have to be efficient.

HORATIO. Hamlet would never have said that.

FORTINBRAS. "Hamlet would never have said that." Loosen up! There's room for more than one philosophy in the world. Is that the right word? Philosophy?

HORATIO. *May I go, sire!?*

FORTINBRAS. Sure, go on. I'm not a tyrant.

HORATIO. *(Starting out, stopping.)* The truth goes beyond death. It can't be changed.

FORTINBRAS. But it can be ignored. Good night, Horatio. *(Horatio exits. As he does so, he passes Osric, entering.)*

OSRIC. My liege —

FORTINBRAS. What is it?

OSRIC. I'm here with tonight's alternatives.

FORTINBRAS. Tonight's alternatives? I totally forgot. Well ... fine, all right. Where are they? *(Osric beckons, and two young Maidens enter. They are clean, but humbly dressed. They stare wide-eyed at the splendors of Elsinore. Fortinbras quickly puts on his crown.)*

OSRIC. Tonight's alternatives.

FORTINBRAS. Is it true, what I've been told?

OSRIC. It is, my liege. They are Polish. *(Nudging them forward.)* Your soldiers brought them back after your last incursion there.

FORTINBRAS. I tell them not to do that. So, do they speak any Danish or Norwegian?

OSRIC. Not a syllable.

FORTINBRAS. How'm I supposed to make them like me?

OSRIC. I really don't know, sire.

FORTINBRAS. Well ... go prepare them.

OSRIC. Both, sire?

FORTINBRAS. Why should I penalize one? *(Osric and the Maidens exit.)* What am I going to do about Horatio? Why won't he *like* me?! Show a guy a little vision, and wham — he seizes up on you. He doesn't even want to talk to me now. Can't get his head out of the past. I hate the past, it's pointless, it's so ... stiff. *(Looking around, to the audience.)* Something about this castle makes me want to talk to myself. Don't know why — I've spent my whole life *not* talking. Out on the battlefield, worried about spies behind every tentflap — all of them working for my uncle. I didn't dare say a word out loud. But here, the minute I'm alone I just ... jabber. *(Suddenly calling out anxiously.)* Osric, where are my alternatives! *(To the audience again.)* I hope you don't think I'm callous, just because of those maidens. They really will have as good a time as can be expected. Under the circumstances. Given the point in history. I'm not known as Fortinbras the Particularly Cruel or anything. I never used to do this sort of thing on my campaigns, but now that I'm King, it's sort of ... expected. And it *has* been a long time. Honest. Not to get too personal. Anyway, I really will try to communicate with them. *(He hears shuffling in the hall.)* At last! *(Polonius appears.)* Not you again.

(Polonius stands attentively, smiles.) Are you going to speak to me tonight? Are you ever going to speak to me? *(Polonius doesn't respond.)* What good is it if you won't tell me anything? *(Polonius shrugs, smiles, moves to the tapestry. He runs his hand over it.)* We keep going through this. What do you want? Do you have a dire warning? Is there a foul injustice? *(At "foul injustice" Polonius becomes excited, as though he wants to speak.)* Yes? *(Polonius suddenly shrugs and waves it off with an "it's not that important" gesture.)* Damn it — ! *(The two Maidens enter in nightdress looking anxiously at Fortinbras.)* What do you want? Oh — sorry. In the bed. *(They follow Fortinbras's gesture and demurely jump into bed. Their wide eyes watch Fortinbras's every move. They do not see Polonius.)* I've got company now, you'll have to go. *(Polonius smiles, remains.)* I'm serious. The alternatives are here. *(No move by Polonius.)* You can't want to watch — you're dead! *(Polonius shrugs.)* This is nuts. *Who sent you?! Why do you appear to me!?* *(Ophelia enters. The Maidens can't see her.)*

OPHELIA.   He always appears where he's least wanted. It's his trademark.

FORTINBRAS.   My God! Lady Ophelia! *(Polonius too looks a bit surprised.)*

OPHELIA.   Yeah, yeah, yeah — Ophelia. Big deal. Who cares? No one did in life — right, Pop?

1st MAIDEN.   *(In Polish, to Fortinbras.)* Are you not well, your highness?

FORTINBRAS.   *(To the Maidens.)* Quiet! *(To Ophelia.)* You spoke.

OPHELIA.   Huzzah. Ring the bells. Ophelia spoke. Of course I spoke. What am I supposed to do? Stand around like him?

FORTINBRAS.   But I thought ghosts —

OPHELIA.   Ghosts do what they like — haven't you figured that out? We're supernatural. Super-natural. Got it? At least, compared to you. *(To Polonius, indicating Fortinbras, rolling her eyes.)* He's King.

2nd MAIDEN.   *(In Polish, worriedly.)* Come to bed, sire.

FORTINBRAS.   *(To the Maidens.)* Can't you see I'm talking?!

OPHELIA.   They can't see us. What on earth are they speaking?

FORTINBRAS. Polish.

OPHELIA. Oh. Wonderful.

FORTINBRAS. Why are you here? Why have you come to me?

OPHELIA. I haven't come to you. I'm just here to collect this old idiot.

FORTINBRAS. But I want him to talk to me.

OPHELIA. You do?

FORTINBRAS. Sure. Ghosts ... know things.

OPHELIA. I'll tell you what ghosts know. They know what they did wrong in life. It's all they can think about. That and a second chance — which never comes. Right, Dad? *(Polonius shrugs.)* Dad talked too much in life. You see where that got him. Now he's afraid to open his mouth. It's really the only good thing I can say about being dead. Hey, Dad — I think I'm still in love with Hamlet. What should I do? *(Polonius fairly burns to advise her, forces himself not to. Ophelia laughs. To Fortinbras.)* Do you really want to know what he's been yearning to say when he comes to see you? The truth — that's all. About anything. When he was alive he couldn't tell the truth even when he tried. Now he won't say anything until he can be absolutely sure it's true. Which, of course, is never. Isn't that right, Dad? *(Cowed, Polonius exits.)* I was the fool in life. Now it's him. Do you remember when we last met?

FORTINBRAS. Yes. You were ... young and fair.

OPHELIA. You saying I'm not now?

FORTINBRAS. No, no. But I guess death is a ... pretty harrowing experience.

OPHELIA. Harrowing. It's been hell on my looks, I'll admit it. *(Suddenly touching him lightly.)* You still look great.

FORTINBRAS. Agh!

1st MAIDEN. *(In Polish.)* Sire?

OPHELIA. Didn't know you could feel me, eh? It usually comes as a shock. I can turn it on and off. Comes in handy. Say, why don't you get rid of them? We can, um ... talk.

FORTINBRAS. Talk?

OPHELIA. Mmm ... unless you're getting other ideas. *(Ophelia turns to the Maidens.)* Come on, girls — everybody up! Go crawl under some other noble. (*Ophelia pulls the cover off the bed. The Maidens scream and exit.*) That's better. (*Climbing onto the bed, pulling the bedcover up around her.*) Are you coming or not?

FORTINBRAS.   You want me to — ?

OPHELIA.   You got it.

FORTINBRAS.   Is it possible?

OPHELIA.   It's not only possible, it's terrific. Did you know women don't reach their sexual peak until after they're dead? (*Fortinbras still can't bring himself to move. Ophelia smiles.*) You're afraid you won't satisfy me, aren't you? Don't worry. You'll still be the only one who ever tried. (*She opens her arms. Fortinbras moves towards the bed. Lights fade to black.*)

Scene 5

Dawn, the next morning. Fortinbras is alone in bed. Kneeling on opposite sides of the bed in a posture of prayer are Gertrude and Claudius. Fortinbras suddenly wakes with a start.

FORTINBRAS.   Ophelia! Don't go, don't — ! (*Noting Claudius and Gertrude.*) Who are you?! (*Suddenly seeing his crown upon Claudius's head, snatching it off.*) Give me that!

CLAUDIUS.   Forgive me. I couldn't help putting it on.

GERTRUDE.   The sin of nostalgia.

CLAUDIUS.   I know. I'm heartily sorry.

GERTRUDE.   Pray with me. (*Gertrude and Claudius instantly fall once more to prayer.*)

FORTINBRAS.   Claudius — !? Gertrude — !? Where's Ophelia? *Where is Ophelia!?*

GERTRUDE.   (*Looking up.*) The sin of wrath.

FORTINBRAS.   Answer my question!

CLAUDIUS.   She left well before daylight. I believe she is a damned soul.

FORTINBRAS.   And you're not?

CLAUDIUS. I have sinned in the past. For which I'm heart-ily sorry.

GERTRUDE. An act of contrition.

CLAUDIUS. In death I am more virtuous.

FORTINBRAS. You have a choice?

GERTRUDE. Everyone has a choice. Dead or alive. I used to think with death would come some sort of final judgment. Then I could embrace my fate, either in heaven or hell, know-ing that I had no choice.

CLAUDIUS. If only it were that easy!

GERTRUDE. Death is harder than life. The temptations we feel are almost irresistible. The lusts —

CLAUDIUS. Don't talk about it!

GERTRUDE. Are only more intense. If I so much as look at Claudius —

CLAUDIUS. Don't look at me!

GERTRUDE. I won't! *(They both avert their gaze.)*

CLAUDIUS. Pray to God!

GERTRUDE. I do!

CLAUDIUS. *(Rushing to his prayer bench.)* The sin of lust! Deliver us from it!

GERTRUDE. Deliver us!

CLAUDIUS. Save us from ourselves!

GERTRUDE. Oh, save us!

FORTINBRAS. *Shut up!! (They fall silent.)* What is wrong with you?!

CLAUDIUS. Everything.

GERTRUDE. We're hideous, hideous beasts. We admit it.

CLAUDIUS. The lust is so intense, but the *remorse* —

GERTRUDE. It's unbearable.

CLAUDIUS. We must be together!

GERTRUDE. But we've got to be apart!

CLAUDIUS. We've come to warn you.

FORTINBRAS. Of what?

GERTRUDE. Ophelia. You had relations with her last night, didn't you?

FORTINBRAS. None of your business.

CLAUDIUS. Fear her.

GERTRUDE. She's a succuba.

FORTINBRAS. And a pretty good one, too!

CLAUDIUS. She will obsess you. She will leap into your heart. She will reach into your spine and travel along every nerve. Your only hunger will be for her. Your only fear will be of her. Your only hope will be in her eyes, and there will be no hope. When you wake in the morning, she will go before you in the day. Every face you see, every hand you touch, every sight, sound, taste, odor — it will all be her.

FORTINBRAS. Have you really looked at Ophelia lately?

CLAUDIUS. I'm not speaking of her appearance!

GERTRUDE. She will mislead you!

CLAUDIUS. She will compound your sin!

FORTINBRAS. What sin?

GERTRUDE. The sin of falsehood!

FORTINBRAS. Falsehood?

GERTRUDE. You buried us in sacred ground!

FORTINBRAS. I thought you'd want to be —

CLAUDIUS. We're sinners! How can we repent?

FORTINBRAS. I don't know —

GERTRUDE. Dig us up — please!!

CLAUDIUS. Throw us on a dungheap!

FORTINBRAS. I'm not listening to another word of this! Get out! Go on! Now!

GERTRUDE. Reject Ophelia!

FORTINBRAS. *Now! (Gertrude and Claudius scramble to their feet and make for an exit. They bump into each other, cry out with alarm and exit separately.)* Geez Louise — this place is overrun. *(Calling after them.)* And don't come back till you're invited! *(Osric enters.)*

OSRIC. My liege.

FORTINBRAS. Osric! You're here early.

OSRIC. I came to fetch last night's alternatives.

FORTINBRAS. Oh. Oh — yes. Well they disappeared. I think there was a ... maidens' meeting of some sort.

OSRIC. I ... see. *(Osric notices the bouquet of dead flowers on the bed, picks them up with a quizzical look.)*

FORTINBRAS. Oh. They wanted to see those. Yesterday

happened to be dead flower day in Poland.

OSRIC. *(Starting out.)* I'll go look for them.

FORTINBRAS. No! Um, no. *(Osric turns.)* Hang around awhile, ok? Make the bed or something. *(Osric does so, hesitantly.)* So, um ... I don't suppose you have any suspects yet? On that Polish spy thing?

OSRIC. No, sire.

FORTINBRAS. Osric — Have you seen any ghosts, ever?

OSRIC. I haven't had that dubious pleasure, sire.

FORTINBRAS. Why dubious? You think ghosts are bad?

OSRIC. Have you seen ghosts?

FORTINBRAS. Me? No. Why should I see ghosts? I mean, do they even exist?

OSRIC. Horatio thinks so.

FORTINBRAS. Well. Horatio.

OSRIC. Indeed.

FORTINBRAS. He and Hamlet saw ghosts everywhere: on the battlements, in the Queen's closet —

OSRIC. I believe they only saw one ghost.

FORTINBRAS. Right. Right — one ghost. That's what I meant. I just thought with so many reported sightings, that maybe you —

OSRIC. I never see ghosts, my liege. They have no need of me.

FORTINBRAS. Need?

OSRIC. Ghosts appear in order to destroy, sire. That's my experience, at least. And I am clearly not worth destroying.

FORTINBRAS. That's not the only reason they appear.

OSRIC. It is, as far as I can tell. Whenever a ghost appears, the next thing I know I'm cleaning up wine stains. *(Fortinbras suddenly grabs a foil from the wall, whirls and grabs Osric by the collar. He pins him to the bed, foil at his throat.)*

FORTINBRAS. *You'll clean up whatever I tell you! Whenever I tell you to, understand?!!*

OSRIC. *My lord Hamlet — !!*

FORTINBRAS. *What?!*

OSRIC. Sorry! Your majesty! Fortinbras! *(Fortinbras lets go of Osric, who falls back on the bed.)*

FORTINBRAS.   What's wrong with me? This isn't like me at all.
OSRIC.   You have seen a ghost!
FORTINBRAS.   Sorry, Osric. I was ... I was up all night. *(Fortinbras exits. Lights fade to black.)*

Scene 6

A cellar in the castle. In the darkness there is a sudden glow. It's a television screen. As it flickers to life, we see no one is onstage. The image on the tv gradually comes into focus. It's a very tight closeup of a man's face. We can see only an angry brow and eye. The eye looks left and right, as though in search of something. We hear the sound of men approaching. Marcellus, Barnardo — bearing torches — rush in, accompanied by Horatio.

MARCELLUS.   This way!
BARNARDO.   I see it! Over here! *(All three stop and stare at the tv from a safe distance. The eye looks in their direction. With great caution, they begin to circle behind it. As they do so, the tv turns with them, so that the eye can continue to watch them. The men make a complete orbit of the tv, and it turns with them the whole way.)*
MARCELLUS.   You see, Horatio. It's as we say.
HORATIO.   I'll speak to it.
BARNARDO.   No! Look what happened last time.
HORATIO.   Who are you? Speak! Reveal yourself! *(The shot on the tv pulls back, revealing the face of Hamlet.)* My lord!
MARCELLUS.   Hamlet!
HORATIO.   *(Falling to his knees.)* Good my lord, speak! Forgive this poor servant. I've failed you in everything. No one knows your story. Fortinbras has put forth a terrible lie —
HAMLET.   Swear.
HORATIO.   M'lord?
HAMLET.   Swear.

HORATIO.   Swear what?

HAMLET.   Swear you'll never touch that button.

HORATIO.   Button? *(Once again, we can see only Hamlet's eye. It jerks once or twice toward a switch on the tv set. Pointing.)* This?

HAMLET.   *DON'T TOUCH IT!!*

HORATIO.   What is it?

BARNARDO.   *(Reading puzzledly.)* "On/off."

HAMLET. *SWEAR!*

HORATIO.   I swear.

MARCELLUS and BARNARDO.   We swear.

HORATIO.   What do you want of us, lord?

HAMLET.   I want ... *(Trailing off.)*

HORATIO.   Yes?

HAMLET.   I want ...

HORATIO.   Anything.

HAMLET.   I want to look at you.

HORATIO.   That's all? Just look at us?

HAMLET.   That's all.

HORATIO.   Of course. For how long?

HAMLET.   *Does it matter!?*

HORATIO.   *(Fearfully.)* No, m'lord! Look at us, by all means. *(Horatio motions the others to kneel with him. They do so.)*

HAMLET.   It's so good to see you. It's all I can do, now: watch and think. I couldn't bring myself to act in life, at least not swiftly enough. Now ...

HORATIO.   Don't blame yourself, m'lord.

HAMLET.   *Who should I blame!?*

HORATIO.   I — I don't know!

HAMLET.   Bring me to Fortinbras.

HORATIO.   My lord?

HAMLET.   *Now. (The three men hurriedly trundle the tv out. Lights fade quickly to black.)*

31

Scene 7

The throne room. Fortinbras sits on the throne, receiving news from Osric. To one side of Fortinbras, apparently invisible to Osric, are Ophelia and Laertes.

FORTINBRAS.   What do you mean we've taken Warsaw? I told the army not to attack.

OSRIC.   They didn't, my liege. They were invited.

FORTINBRAS.   Invited?

OPHELIA.   I told you you were popular.

OSRIC.   Apparently the Poles, seeing our combined armies on their border, decided to forestall further hostilities by surrendering unconditionally.

FORTINBRAS.   But they don't even know what we want.

OPHELIA.   *(To Laertes.)* What do we want?

OSRIC.   We'll have to want something, sire.

FORTINBRAS.   Well, I don't know — maybe we should have the troops stay in Warsaw for awhile and ... mingle.

OSRIC.   Mingle?

FORTINBRAS.   Not possible, eh? What's wrong with me? I used to be so decisive.

OPHELIA.   Maybe you're not getting enough sleep.

LAERTES.   Ophelia — !

OPHELIA.   Oh, bite it, Laertes.

FORTINBRAS.   Well ... have the army declare victory then, and ... just come back.

OSRIC.   Yes, sire.

FORTINBRAS.   And have them tell the Poles to ... watch it.

OSRIC.   Very well, sire.

OPHELIA.   *(To Fortinbras.)* I love it when you're stern. *(Osric turns to go. Before he can do so, the Captain enters and falls to one knee. He too is unable to see Ophelia or Laertes.)*

CAPTAIN.   My liege.

FORTINBRAS.   What is it?

CAPTAIN.   The army's left Warsaw — they're pushing on.

FORTINBRAS.   Pushing on?

CAPTAIN. Yes, sire — towards Carpathia.

FORTINBRAS. Carpathia?

OSRIC. Just beyond Poland, quite mountainous — nice in the summer.

FORTINBRAS. I know where it is! Why are they doing that?

CAPTAIN. No one knows. But most of the Polish army has joined them.

FORTINBRAS. I can't have this. This is all wrong. Get them back. Tell them to come home. Now!

CAPTAIN. *(Exiting.)* Yes, sire.

FORTINBRAS. *(To Ophelia and Laertes.)* Carpathia. The minute my generals get back, you guys are going to have company.

OSRIC. Sire, to whom are you speaking?

FORTINBRAS. *(Defensively.)* Nobody.

OSRIC. Of course, sire.

FORTINBRAS. What about the Polish spy?

OSRIC. The — ? Oh ... no progress, I'm afraid.

FORTINBRAS. Why not?

OSRIC. I wasn't aware that you wanted progress. And then there's the fact that there is no actual ... spy.

FORTINBRAS. We have to have a spy now. After a victory like this? With no shots being fired? We need a reason to have gone at all. A villain.

OSRIC. But sire —

FORTINBRAS. One Polish spy. An opponent. This is all about self-image, Osric. How can we be heroes if we can't even see who we've triumphed over? We need someone we can hate right here, right now. Someone palpable. A volunteer, maybe. What about you?

OSRIC. Me?

FORTINBRAS. Yeah, what are you doing?

OSRIC. Well ... nothing, but —

FORTINBRAS. That's a great idea! You'd be perfect! Believe me, I wouldn't ask if it wasn't important. The public needs this kind of image right now. You know? A human face we can all loathe and detest. Your face.

OSRIC. I don't know ...

FORTINBRAS. What do you mean, you don't know? We need a Polish spy, and you're elected. It's simple as that. Understand?

OSRIC. But ... but ... *(Fortinbras stares at Osric.)* Very well.

FORTINBRAS. Good! Thanks. *(An awkward beat.)*

OSRIC. So ... I'll just ... go put myself ... in jail. *(Osric exits. Ophelia instantly kisses Fortinbras hard.)*

LAERTES. Ophelia — !

OPHELIA. *(Ending the kiss, to Laertes.)* Why are you hanging around, anyway? Did Claudius and Gertrude send you?

FORTINBRAS. Sometimes I wonder how well I'm running the government.

OPHELIA. You're doing fine. You just had a great victory. Let's celebrate. *(She snuggles up to Fortinbras.)*

FORTINBRAS. Stop that — we're in public.

OPHELIA. You mean *you're* in public.

FORTINBRAS. For God's sake — your brother's here.

OPHELIA. So what? He wants me too.

LAERTES. *Ophelia — !*

OPHELIA. Don't be such a phoney — admit it. Like it matters anymore. *(To Fortinbras.)* Sometimes I don't think he even knows he's dead.

LAERTES. It came as such a shock —

OPHELIA. That's what happens when you think you're immortal. You should've been raised as a girl. Then you'd have been ready. *(She reaches for Fortinbras again. He moves away.)*

FORTINBRAS. *Please* — ! I'm just feeling disoriented right now, ok? Having a ghost for a ...

OPHELIA. For a what? Say it. For a lover.

FORTINBRAS. I don't know what I'm feeling. Or if I'm feeling anything. Or if there's anything to *feel.*

OPHELIA. *(Placing Fortinbras's hand on a provocative part of her anatomy.)* Feel this.

LAERTES. *Ophelia — !*

OPHELIA. Oh, grab it while you can. Get 'em while they're living — that's what I say. *(She kisses Fortinbras again.)*

LAERTES. Fortinbras? Fortinbras — I appeal to you. If you don't respect the boundary between the living and the dead,

34

how can you expect us to?

OPHELIA.   Boundaries are made to be broken. *(Fortinbras pulls away.)*

FORTINBRAS.   Osric said all ghosts come to destroy.

OPHELIA.   Osric? Osric the Wise?

FORTINBRAS.   How do I know he's not right?

OPHELIA.   Well, you did look pretty destroyed last night.

FORTINBRAS.   That's not what I mean. How do I know you're not going to win me to my doom?

OPHELIA.   Oh, that is *sweet!* Win you to your doom. You are so cute sometimes. *(She kisses him again.)*

LAERTES.   Fortinbras? Wouldn't you rather go kick a ball around or something? It's a beautiful day. I feel athletic.

OPHELIA.   *(Coming up for air.)* Me too. *(They go back into the clinch. Unnoticed by the three of them, Horatio wheels in the tv, complete with its image of Hamlet's eye. Horatio can't see Ophelia or Laertes.)*

HORATIO.   Sire?

FORTINBRAS.   What? Oh — Horatio!

HORATIO.   Why did you have your tongue out, sire?

FORTINBRAS.   Never mind! What's this?

HORATIO.   I found it in the cellar, sire. It's Prince Hamlet.

FORTINBRAS.   Hamlet?

HORATIO.   Well ... his ghost.

FORTINBRAS.   *Another* one?

HORATIO.   Sire?

FORTINBRAS.   *(Of the tv.)* What's he doing in there?

HORATIO.   It's a minor inhibition. We're still working on it. If you'll just listen to what he —

FORTINBRAS.   No! No — I refuse. No more ghosts! This is my castle now, my kingdom. It's my army in ... in ...

OPHELIA.   Carpathia.

FORTINBRAS.   Carpathia! I'm not going to be distracted or betrayed by any more ghosts!

HORATIO.   *(Seeing only Hamlet.)* *More* ghosts? But there's only ...

FORTINBRAS.   You're dead! You understand?! You're all

dead, and I'm free of you! From this moment on! You hear me? Free! *(Fortinbras storms out, with Laertes following.)*

LAERTES. You want to kick a ball around?

FORTINBRAS. *NO!!* *(Fortinbras and Laertes are gone.)*

HORATIO. *(Looking around, puzzled.)* Carpathia? Who else does he see? *(To the tv.)* I'm sorry, m'lord — he's gone.

HAMLET. You've done well. Leave me now.

HORATIO. Leave you?

HAMLET. *Go!* *(Horatio hurries out.)*

OPHELIA. So. You found your way back.

HAMLET. Is Claudius here?

OPHELIA. Yeah, he didn't have any trouble. Funny, eh? Looks like you're in a fix.

HAMLET. I want to be back. Among you.

OPHELIA. So? Get out of the box.

HAMLET. I don't know how! Please — I have so much to do.

OPHELIA. Don't worry. I'm doing it for you. Fortinbras is completely under my control.

HAMLET. He's not telling the truth!

OPHELIA. He's been busy. Conquering Poland.

HAMLET. Help me!

OPHELIA. Do I look like I have a manual? I don't know how to help you. What's this? "On/off"?

HAMLET. *Don't touch that! Free me, Ophelia!*

OPHELIA. Why should I?

FORTINBRAS. *Free me now, as you love me! Ophe — !!* *(Ophelia turns off the set.)*

OPHELIA. Dream on. *(She starts out, stops.)* God, that felt good. *(Ophelia exits. Lights fade slowly to black. Just as they reach black, the tv turns on again, by itself. We see the brooding eye of Hamlet. Then darkness.)*

END OF ACT ONE

ACT TWO

Scene 1

A castle hall. Polonius appears. He carries with him the Queen's old tapestry. He stops, looks around to make sure no one's there. Satisfied, he spreads out the tapestry, finds the hole made by Hamlet's sword.

POLONIUS.   *(Touching it.)* Here. *(Touching his chest.)* Here. *(To the audience.)* It does something to a man's point of view when he suddenly feels a sword go through his heart. I was pinned like a bug against the wall. Where was all my good advice then? Stuck in my throat, where it's remained ever since. Oh, I still have plenty of advice, don't misunderstand. I could tell everybody in this castle, living and dead, what to do. But to hell with 'em, that's what I say. *(Sighing.)* If there were a hell. There doesn't seem to be, for me. No heaven either, that I've been able to discern. Only this — wandering around the scene of all my errors, watching everyone make the same old mistakes, *burning* to advise them — and hating myself for it. Death has been my greatest disappointment. It's too much like life. I thought there would be a great adventure, but there's no great adventure. I've asked the King, the Queen, the others — no one's had a great adventure. So far, there's been nothing to compare with that first moment, pinned against a wall, translated by a steel point — my face buried against the blank side of a tapestry — hoping that in a single instant all might finally be revealed. *(Tossing over the corner of the tapestry.)* What a hoax. Death has all the uncertainty of life, and twice the solitude. If you take my advice — and no one ever does — you'll avoid it. *(Polonius turns to go. As he does, Fortinbras steps into view. Polonius freezes.)*
FORTINBRAS.   You spoke! *(Polonius turns and hurries toward another exit. Fortinbras moves to block his way.)* No, you don't! Talk to me — now! *(Polonius tries another direction. Fortinbras*

blocks him again.) Can't you see how desperate I am?! *(Polonius tries yet another direction. Fortinbras doesn't move.)* Damn it, I need your *advice! (Polonius stops, fighting his urge to advise. Fortinbras falls to his knees.)* Please! Nothing makes sense anymore. I swore off ghosts, I even swore off Ophelia. But I can't make it stick! Every time I see her, I just crumble. I used to handle everything so well: battles, intrigues, women. I never even worked up a sweat. But here at Elsinore I've seen things — I've *done* things.... Give me advice, Polonius, please! One sentence, one phrase, one word.

POLONIUS.   Ophelia.

FORTINBRAS.   Ophelia?

POLONIUS.   Lay off her.

FORTINBRAS.   Ok — ok. I know I should. Why?

POLONIUS.   It's obvious. You're not suited to treat with the dead. Hamlet was fathoms deeper than you. Now look at him: locked in a box of light — and he only *talked* to a ghost.

FORTINBRAS.   What you're saying is, I'm in jeopardy here.

POLONIUS.   At least.

FORTINBRAS.   But I have these feelings about her. It's not like with any other girl.

POLONIUS.   I should hope not.

FORTINBRAS.   It's so *intense.* The minute I see her, the minute I touch her —

POLONIUS.   I *am* her father.

FORTINBRAS.   It's love. How can I resist that?

POLONIUS.   What you feel isn't love, it's nostalgia. For non-existence.

FORTINBRAS.   For non — ?

POLONIUS.   The moment we become aware of our own existence, we secretly begin to long for the time before: when we never were. And why not? It's attractive — utter oblivion, utter peace. *Non-being.* We think death will give us that again. No wonder we fall in love with it. But that's not what death gives us. Nothing can erase, completely, what has been.

FORTINBRAS.   So, um — how would I fit that into a plan of action?

POLONIUS.   Tell the truth! To thine own self be —

FORTINBRAS. Nice?

POLONIUS. *TRUE!!*

FORTINBRAS. Right.

POLONIUS. And get married!

FORTINBRAS. To Ophelia?

POLONIUS. No, not to Ophelia! To someone else.

FORTINBRAS. Who?

POLONIUS. It doesn't matter. Someone living, that's all.

FORTINBRAS. Married? But there's no one.

POLONIUS. What about those two I saw in your bed?

FORTINBRAS. They were just — They don't even speak my language.

POLONIUS. All the better! Find them. Marry one. Then maybe Ophelia will leave you alone, and you can gain the courage to tell the truth.

FORTINBRAS. About *what?* What truth am I supposed to tell?

POLONIUS. Hamlet's truth. My truth. Without it, nothing can go forward — all is held back.

FORTINBRAS. But I've already told the Polish spy story —

POLONIUS. *Tell the truth!!* What did I just tell you?!

FORTINBRAS. But —

POLONIUS. *You can't take advice! None of you! You never take advice!!* I'm leaving.

FORTINBRAS. No — ! *(Polonius starts out, dragging the tapestry behind him. Fortinbras grabs a corner of it.)* What should I do about the army? They took Carpathia without a shot!

POLONIUS. *(Tugging at the tapestry.)* I don't care!

FORTINBRAS. Why's Hamlet in a box?

POLONIUS. Let go!

FORTINBRAS. Should I hang Osric?

POLONIUS. *I don't care!! (Polonius tugs the arras free.)* Tell the truth. Tell it soon. There isn't much time — for either of us.

FORTINBRAS. What do you mean? You're dead.

POLONIUS. You think eternity's forever? *(Polonius exits. Fortinbras stares after him. Fortinbras exits the opposite way. A moment passes, then Horatio hurries in, pushing Osric ahead of him. Osric is in chains.)*

OSRIC.   Horatio, stop it! Where are you taking me!?
HORATIO.   Quiet.
OSRIC.   I won't be quiet! You're hurting me! Horatio — !
(Managing to pull away.) Put me back in my cell.
HORATIO.   No.
OSRIC.   I demand it!
HORATIO.   I'm trying to save your life!
OSRIC.   Why?
HORATIO.   *Why!?*
OSRIC.   It's none of your business. Besides, you don't even
like me.
HORATIO.   I *need* you! We're the only ones who know the
truth. Do you want to hang? *(Osric is silent. Horatio pushes him
along again. Osric resists.)*
OSRIC.   Where is it we're going?
HORATIO.   I'm getting you out of the castle. *(Osric is
stunned.)*
OSRIC.   Out of the — ? Out of — ?!
HORATIO.   What's wrong?
OSRIC.   I've never ... I've never ...
HORATIO.   What!?
OSRIC.   *Been* out of the castle. *(Now Horatio is stunned.)*
HORATIO.   Never?
OSRIC.   There was no need. Everything I wanted was right
here. Out there it was all just ... Denmark.
HORATIO.   *(Pushing him again.)* You'll get used to it.
OSRIC.   No, no, no, no, no — Horatio — please! Just stop!
Stop for a minute and *listen to me!* (Horatio stops.) I want to
hang.
HORATIO.   What?
OSRIC.   That's overstated. But I would rather hang than
have to go out into ... whatever that is. I've seen it from the
ramparts, Horatio. No one looks happy out there. No one's
well dressed —
HORATIO.   *(Pushing him yet again.)* Come on.
OSRIC.   *I'm a Polish spy!! Listen, everyone! I'm a spy! I really
am!!*
HORATIO.   Shut up.

OSRIC. *Long live Poland!*

HORATIO. *(Clapping a hand over Osric's mouth.)* You're insane! Everyone in this castle is. *(Osric nods.)* How can you accept it? You've been falsely accused. Even you must feel some outrage.

OSRIC. Outrage is a luxury best enjoyed by those who can do something about it. I must simply be patient and wait for the storm to pass over me.

HORATIO. Or swallow you whole.

OSRIC. No system's perfect. May I please go back to my cell now?

HORATIO. All right. Till I can think of another way. But don't blame me if you're hanged in the meantime. Fair enough?

OSRIC. You are good to me, Horatio.

HORATIO. I'm just trying to do one honest thing.

OSRIC. We all have our faults. *(Horatio pushes Osric off the way they came. Lights fade to black.)*

Scene 2

Lights slowly come up on the Queen's chambers. As they do, we hear the following, which starts in darkness.

CLAUDIUS. My words fly up, my thoughts remain below —

HAMLET. Kill him!

CLAUDIUS. My words fly up —

HAMLET. Kill him! Kill him now!

CLAUDIUS. My words —

HAMLET. *What are you waiting for? (By now lights are up. They reveal Claudius kneeling at his prayer bench. Laertes stands behind him with a drawn dagger. In the foreground Gertrude lies on the now-familiar tapestry, in an awkward — if alluring — posture. U., surveying all this, is Hamlet — or Hamlet's eye, rather — since he's still in the tv.)*

LAERTES. I — I can't.

41

HAMLET.   Why not?

CLAUDIUS.   Am I facing the wrong way? Maybe if I —

LAERTES.   No, no — it's just that this isn't what happened.

HAMLET.   It's what should have happened. Go on — kill him! He won't feel a thing.

CLAUDIUS.   Only remorse.

LAERTES.   But it's so meaningless. I won't be sending him to heaven *or* hell. We're all just floating here. I don't understand why we had to carry all this stuff into the Queen's chamber in the first place. Feels weird.

HAMLET.   Never mind that.

LAERTES.   Besides, I'm not really a man of violence.

HAMLET.   Neither was I. *(Claudius laughs.)* Quiet! As long as I'm confined to this box, I'll spend my time as I like! Now strike, Laertes! While the chance is there!

GERTRUDE.   Please strike, Laertes. This is such a humiliating posture.

HAMLET.   You be quiet, too! Claudius — again!

CLAUDIUS.   My words fly up, my thoughts remain —

HAMLET.   Now, Laertes! *(Laertes stabs Claudius, who gives a mortal groan.)* Yes! *(Claudius falls to the floor, dies.)* How easy it was! How exquisite! If only I'd really done it!

LAERTES.   Why didn't you?

CLAUDIUS.   *(Rising, kneeling at the bench.)* Yes, why didn't you?

GERTRUDE.   Why didn't you?

HAMLET.   Quiet! All of you! Laertes, stab him again.

LAERTES.   But I just —

HAMLET.   You heard me! I want to see it again!

CLAUDIUS.   It's all right. I deserve it. A thousandfold, if you like.

GERTRUDE.   This is so uncomfortable — can't we get to my part?

CLAUDIUS.   Yes, do her part.

HAMLET.   Very well. Begin.

GERTRUDE.   Please forgive me my son, for all the wrongs I've committed.

HAMLET.   Such as?

GERTRUDE.   Lusting after Claudius.

HAMLET.   And?

GERTRUDE.   Marrying him so soon after he murdered your father.

HAMLET.   And?

GERTRUDE.   Not giving you my whole support.

HAMLET.   *And?*

GERTRUDE.   Don't make me say it.

HAMLET.   Say it! It's the truth!

GERTRUDE.   And forgive me for lusting after you.

HAMLET.   *Yes!*

LAERTES.   She — !? I never knew that.

GERTRUDE.   It's not true.

HAMLET.   It is! You wanted me. Just as I wanted you. The unspeakable attraction. The root cause of all our sufferings.

CLAUDIUS.   I thought I was the root cause.

HAMLET.   *The root cause is what I say it is!!* (*They fall to arguing. Ophelia enters, topping all their voices.*)

OPHELIA.   *What is going on in here?* I can hear you from across the cas — (*Stopping short as she takes in the scene; with disgust.*) Oh, very nice.

HAMLET.   Get out of here.

OPHELIA.   (*To Hamlet.*) This was your idea, I suppose. You are such an infant.

HAMLET.   It's none of your business.

OPHELIA.   Your mother's bedroom. How old are you?

HAMLET.   What's between me and my mother —

OPHELIA.   Is really nauseating, I know.

HAMLET.   *Get thee to a —* !

OPHELIA.   (*Suddenly pointing a remote control at the tv.*) Shut up. (*Hamlet's mouth continues to move, but we hear no sound. To the others.*) Isn't that nice? (*She turns up the sound again.*)

HAMLET.   ... just a horny little lady-in-waiting with ambitions above her — (*She turns the sound off. Hamlet's mouth keeps working. After a moment she turns the sound on again.*) ... don't think you went mad at all. You probably *tripped* into the river —

OPHELIA.   (*Turning the sound off again.*) I could do this all day. (*She turns the sound back up.*)

HAMLET.   Where did you get that?

OPHELIA.   In the cellar. Neat, eh?

HAMLET.   Laertes — take it away from her!

OPHELIA.   Don't worry. I won't abuse it. Go ahead, show me what you're doing here. I could use the laugh.

HAMLET.   Yes! Yes — good idea. Let's show her. *(Claudius, Gertrude and Laertes all groan tiredly.)*

LAERTES.   *Hamlet ...*

HAMLET.   *Do it! Now! (They reluctantly resume their positions. Ophelia looks on.)* All right! Kill him again!

CLAUDIUS.   My words fly up —

HAMLET.   Kill him! Keep stabbing! And mother — writhe! *(Laertes stabs Claudius over and over. Claudius doesn't fall, but groans mightily each time. Gertrude writhes demurely on the tapestry.)*

GERTRUDE.   Hamlet, I want you! God forgive me, I want you so!

HAMLET.   *Yes! Yes!! Yes!!! YES!! YES!!!! (A sudden darkness, followed by an explosion of light and smoke. Almost immediately lights rise again to reveal the same scene. Hamlet stands beside an empty tv. The others are surprised.)*

GERTRUDE.   Hamlet!

HAMLET.   *(Smiling.)* I thought that might do the trick.

LAERTES.   Well ... um, welcome back.

HAMLET.   Thanks. I'm sorry for some of the things I've made you all do, but I thought if I could just let myself go —

GERTRUDE.   We don't mind.

CLAUDIUS.   Whatever works for you.

HAMLET.   No hard feelings?

CLAUDIUS.   No, no, no.

LAERTES.   *(Simultaneously.)* No problem.

GERTRUDE.   *(Simultaneously.)* Not at all. *(Hamlet looks at Ophelia.)*

HAMLET.   And you? *(Ophelia approaches Hamlet slowly, aiming the remote control at him. Suddenly she lets it fall to the floor and melts into a deep romantic kiss with him. Lights fade to black.)*

Scene 3

The throne room. Fortinbras sits despondently on his throne as Horatio reads from a parchment.

HORATIO.   After the conquest of Carpathia, the combined Danish and Norwegian ... and Polish and Carpathian forces have successfully placed Transylvania, Anatolia and the Trans-Caucasus under your control. *(Fortinbras gives little groans at each new name.)* No hand has been raised in anger. No battles have been fought. In each case, the swelling hordes were welcomed as heroes of liberation, ushering in peace, prosperity, enlightenment — etc., etc. Shall I go on?

FORTINBRAS.   No.

HORATIO.   *(With a glance at the parchment.)* Apparently they are.

FORTINBRAS.   What's happening, Horatio? What's happening to me?

HORATIO.   You're winning.

FORTINBRAS.   Why don't I feel like I'm winning?

HORATIO.   I'm sure it's hard for you to know, without —

FORTINBRAS.   Without what?

HORATIO.   I was going to say, without speaking to my lord Hamlet.

FORTINBRAS.   I won't talk to Hamlet! That's final!

HORATIO.   But his *story* —

FORTINBRAS.   It's too late for his story! We're committed now. Troops are in the field. Troops are in *all* the fields.

HORATIO.   But he could teach you —

FORTINBRAS.   This is no time for an education! I can't get caught up in ethics, for God's sake.

HORATIO.   We're beyond ethics now. More in the realm of first causes, the nature of being, phenomenology, metaphysics —

FORTINBRAS.   Don't talk metaphysics to me! I've been sleeping with a dead woman!

HORATIO.   Pardon?

45

FORTINBRAS. Ophelia. She's back. So are the rest of them. Hamlet's not the only ghost — they're all here. Especially Ophelia.

HORATIO. You and Ophelia are — ? *(Fortinbras nods.)* And you won't even *talk* to Hamlet?

FORTINBRAS. I suppose you think it's unnatural. Decadent. Perverted.

HORATIO. It's ... out of the ordinary.

FORTINBRAS. Well, it's over. I'm not seeing her anymore. Satisfied?

HORATIO. I ... I don't —

FORTINBRAS. She used to affect my judgment. I can see it now. I lost my edge.

HORATIO. Speaking of judgments — you've condemned Osric.

FORTINBRAS. I had to; he's a spy.

HORATIO. But — not really.

FORTINBRAS. What do you mean, not really? Didn't you read the proclamation?

HORATIO. Yes, sire. But you know and I know —

FORTINBRAS. Besides, I commuted his sentence.

HORATIO. I don't think a commutation from being whipped to death to hanging is really —

FORTINBRAS. You want me to be *more* merciful?

HORATIO. I think you should release him.

FORTINBRAS. Release him?! What did I send him to prison for?

HORATIO. I don't know, my liege. Perhaps this ghost of Lady Ophelia you describe —

FORTINBRAS. You're saying my political judgment's being influenced by a woman?

HORATIO. You just said so yourself.

FORTINBRAS. I did? Right — I did. Well, don't worry. I'm taking steps to correct the situation. I'm getting married.

HORATIO. Married? To whom?

FORTINBRAS. To one of those Polish girls, if I can find them again. They seem to have gotten misplaced. And if they're still alive. Otherwise the wedding's off.

HORATIO.   In any case, I think you should release Osric. Clearly you condemned him at a time when you were ... were ...

FORTINBRAS.   Crazy? Is that what you're trying to say?

HORATIO.   Actually, I'm trying *not* to say it —

FORTINBRAS.   Well, consider it said. After Hamlet, you must think every Prince is crazy, but it's not true. I can function. I can make calm, rational judgments. Just watch: A.) I'm releasing Osric —

HORATIO.   Thank you, my sovereign!

FORTINBRAS.   Probably too late for a Polish spy by now, anyway. We'll start looking for a spy from wherever the army is at the moment.

HORATIO.   *(Consulting his parchment.)* Umm — Persia.

FORTINBRAS.   Persia?! Fine. B.) I'm ordering the army home again, not that they'll listen. And C.) I'm going to marry a living Polish woman as soon as possible in order to be no longer distracted by a ghost who was admittedly magnificent in bed.

HORATIO.   This is very kingly.

FORTINBRAS.   Thought you'd like that. It's not so hard to be regal. I could do it all the time, if I liked. So, go! Send word to the army!

HORATIO.   Yes, sire! *(Horatio starts out, stops.)* Sire, this is not only kingly of you. It's very ... educated.

FORTINBRAS.   *(Complemented.)* Yeah? Thanks. *(Horatio exits. The Captain rushes in, goes to one knee.)*

CAPTAIN.   My liege.

FORTINBRAS.   What is it?

CAPTAIN.   There's been an explosion in the Queen's quarters.

FORTINBRAS.   Explosion? Was anyone hurt?

CAPTAIN.   No one was found at all. Only a strange sort of ... box.

FORTINBRAS.   Box? *(Gesturing.)* Was it about ... this big?

CAPTAIN.   Yes, my liege.

FORTINBRAS.   And it was empty?

CAPTAIN.   Quite empty.

FORTINBRAS.   Oh, *great*. Hamlet's out!

CAPTAIN.   My liege?

FORTINBRAS.   Oh, nothing. Have you found the two Polish maidens?

CAPTAIN.   Not yet, sire.

FORTINBRAS.   Find them! I'm in constant danger until I marry one of them. Oh — and I almost forgot — release Osric from his suffering. At once!

CAPTAIN.   Release — ? My liege! *(The Captain exits.)*

FORTINBRAS.   I'm feeling a little better already. It's good to put some discipline into your life. If I can just get the army to tone it down.... But I'm more in control. More than ever. Horatio's right. There *is* something educated about not executing innocent people. It's not as workable, but it's ... more relaxed. Not to mention controlling your urges to sleep with the dead. Polonius was *really* right about that. *(With sudden, panicky fury.) Where are those Polish maidens?!! I can't wait forever!! (Regaining an intense calm.)* I have total control. Nothing bothers me. Not even Hamlet. Oh, I know the whispers'll start, now that he's out of that box. "Hamlet would've been a better king. Hamlet would've known what to do. Hamlet had more depth." *(Shouting, as before.) Well, Hamlet's dead, if anybody hasn't noticed!! Hamlet's dead and I'm alive — there's a big difference!! (Quieter.)* I wonder where he is? He could be anywhere. He could be here. Is that it? Are you here, watching me? Laughing at my mistakes? What if you are? Kings don't make mistakes, anyway. They reassess policies. *(A sudden realization.)* What if he's not here at all? What if he's promulgating his story? All over the castle? What if he's telling the truth, and people are ... *believing* it? No, no — stop. Just stop! Get hold of yourself. It's what the King says that matters. Just keep the story *straight*. A spy — of indeterminate nationality. A plot, mass-regicide, sacred ground. It's the only logical story. The only ... logical ... *(Unable to help himself, shouting running out of the room.)* Hamlet! *Hamlet!!* *(He exits. Lights fade to black.)*

Scene 4

The battlements. Hamlet and Ophelia sit together staring out over the landscape. She leans against him. They are holding hands. Behind them, at a distance, are Marcellus and Barnardo, quietly watching the two ghosts.

OPHELIA.   Things seem so simple suddenly. Why do you think we had so much trouble before?

HAMLET.   Who knows? We were just a pair of kids. Who had the perspective? *(She sighs, resting her head on his shoulder. He looks at Marcellus and Barnardo.)* Why are Marcellus and Barnardo over there?

OPHELIA.   Fortinbras is trying to avoid me. He's assigned them to keep watch whenever I appear.

HAMLET.   Oh. *(Marcellus and Barnardo smile.)*

OPHELIA.   We could've been so happy. Married, children — waiting for Claudius and Gertrude to die.

HAMLET.   Yeah, it sounds good, doesn't it? Well, it can't always work out, trying to make the best decision in life.

OPHELIA.   You didn't make any. *(Hamlet looks at her.)* Hardly any. You finally managed to kill Claudius, but you had to clean out the whole castle to do it.

HAMLET.   If by that you mean I was careful to examine all the moral ramifications of an act of personal revenge —

OPHELIA.   I mean you stalled around, and acted like a lunatic, and generally let things get worse and worse, that's all. And you killed my father.

HAMLET.   That was an accident.

OPHELIA.   And my brother.

HAMLET.   He killed me.

OPHELIA.   Anyway, all I'm saying is, you took an awfully long time to do a very simple thing. Badly.

HAMLET.   *(Starting to leave.)* If that's how you feel about it —

OPHELIA.   No, no, no — oh, Hamlet, no! I didn't mean it! Hold me, please just hold —

HAMLET.   *(Simultaneously, falling into an embrace with her.)*

Ophelia — !

OPHELIA. We've been through so much together; we can't fight anymore, we can't!

HAMLET. You're right!

OPHELIA. Say that again. Please?

HAMLET. Ophelia, you're right.

OPHELIA. *(With a sigh of pleasure.)* Oh! *(They kiss. Marcellus and Barnardo look on attentively. When the kiss ends, Hamlet looks at them. They avert their gaze. Ophelia and Hamlet stare off over the fields.)*

HAMLET. You know, it all began right here.

OPHELIA. What?

HAMLET. My father's ghost. This is where I saw him — promenading through the air at midnight, just beyond this wall.

OPHELIA. We could do that; would you like to?

HAMLET. No, that's all right. It makes me think about everything that's happened. I can hardly wait till Horatio convinces Fortinbras to let the real story come out.

OPHELIA. You ... think he will?

HAMLET. Of course. Inevitably. The truth will out.

OPHELIA. But would that really be good?

HAMLET. What do you mean? Of course — why wouldn't it be?

OPHELIA. I don't come off particularly well in the real story. I mean, I tend to look sort of like ... an idiot.

HAMLET. I was cruel, I admit. But —

OPHELIA. Does it really matter what people think?

HAMLET. Of course it matters. What do you think we all suffered and died for?

OPHELIA. Nothing, in my case. Please, Hamlet — let things stay as they are. We have each other, at last. We can be content with that.

HAMLET. Maybe you can, but ... not me.

OPHELIA. Hamlet — ! I can't believe you won't do this one little thing for me.

HAMLET. Little?! My whole reputation? My *story?* The mark I made in the world. The great lesson I have to teach.

OPHELIA.   What? Stab quicker?

HAMLET.   I might have expected you not to understand.

OPHELIA.   Because I'm a girl — right. You haven't changed a bit! I'm going back to Fortinbras.

HAMLET.   You don't love me at all, do you? This has simply been a contemptible ruse. You're trying to use me.

OPHELIA.   Oh, *there's* a shock! One of us trying to use the other. I wonder if that's ever happened before?

HAMLET.   The story will be told!

OPHELIA.   From whose point of view? Yours? Mr. Hamlet It's-All-About-Me the Dane? Oh, sure — your point of view is clearly the most rewarding, the most complex. No wonder it has a special right to exist.

HAMLET.   Ophelia —

OPHELIA.   *I will not ... be ... marginal!*

HAMLET.   I thought by now you'd understand. I thought when you committed suicide —

OPHELIA.   I didn't commit suicide, I was pushed!

HAMLET.   By whom?

OPHELIA.   By your mother.

HAMLET.   That's a disgraceful lie!

OPHELIA.   *Were you there?!* If Fortinbras can tell a new story, so can I. *(Fortinbras rushes in, stopping short when he sees Ophelia.)*

FORTINBRAS.   *Ophelia!!*

OPHELIA.   Fortinbras?!

FORTINBRAS.   I'll ... come back later.

OPHELIA.   No — *wait!* I haven't said hello yet. *(Clearly for Hamlet's benefit, Ophelia gives Fortinbras a very memorable kiss. Hamlet pulls out a dagger and moves to strike Fortinbras with it in the back. Barnardo and Marcellus stare horrified. But Hamlet can't bring himself to strike the blow, and instead stalks out of the room. Fortinbras breaks the kiss.)*

FORTINBRAS.   No ... no ... I — thank you, but — actually I just came to make sure that Hamlet's been behaving. You know — about everything.

OPHELIA.   He's not.

FORTINBRAS.   He's not? Oh. Well ... maybe I'd better go

find him, then. And about the kissing — I can't actually, any-more, because I'm about to get married.

OPHELIA.   To whom?

FORTINBRAS.   Uh ... someone Polish. I'll just be on my way now, ok? So ... 'bye. *(He starts out.)*

OPHELIA.   *Wait right there! (Fortinbras stops.)* Are you saying my kiss doesn't do anything for you?

FORTINBRAS.   Of course. It does too much! That's the whole problem.

OPHELIA.   I'll tell you what the problem is. The problem is you and Hamlet. Sure, Ophelia's fine for a good time now and then, but the minute you have another priority, Ophelia goes right out the window!

FORTINBRAS.   No, you don't...!

OPHELIA.   Listen to me — don't get married!

FORTINBRAS.   I have to.

OPHELIA.   If you love me, you won't!

FORTINBRAS.   *(Torn, but resolute.)* I'm sorry.

OPHELIA.   *(Storming out.) Oh — why can't someone just kiss me and do what I want?!!!*

FORTINBRAS.   *(With a look at Marcellus and Barnardo.)* You guys are a *great* help! *(He exits. Lights fade to black.)*

Scene 5

A hall in the castle. Claudius and Gertrude are on their knees praying silently, heads bowed, with the two Maidens. Fortinbras hurries in, looking behind him and muttering. Neither he nor the four praying notice each other at first.

FORTINBRAS.   *(To himself.)* She had no right to yell at me. No right at all. I am through with ghosts forever, and that's — ! *(Fortinbras falls over Claudius.)* Agh!

MAIDENS.   Oh!!

GERTRUDE.   Your majesty — !

CLAUDIUS.   *(Helping him up.)* Are you all right? I'm heartily sorry!

FORTINBRAS. *(Slapping his hand away.)* I'm fine! I'm fine! Leave me alone! *(With surprise.)* The maidens!!!

GERTRUDE. We asked them to pray with us.

CLAUDIUS. They seemed to need it.

FORTINBRAS. You let them see you? You could've terrorized them!

GERTRUDE. They don't know who we are.

CLAUDIUS. They don't even know we're dead.

FORTINBRAS. And no one's going to tell them! Get out!

GERTRUDE. Again?

FORTINBRAS. I have things to do!

CLAUDIUS. There's something you should know about these maidens —

FORTINBRAS. I know what I need to know. Go!

CLAUDIUS. You'll be surprised —

FORTINBRAS. *Out! (Gertrude and Claudius exit — separately. To the Maidens.)* So. Praying. That's lovely. That's very ... maidenlike. *(Suddenly remembering.)* Why am I talking to you? You don't speak a word.

1st MAIDEN. *(With a strong accent.)* You ... want it bad?

FORTINBRAS. What?

2nd MAIDEN. *(With an accent.)* Hot time ... my stud?

FORTINBRAS. How do you...? How can you...?

1st MAIDEN. I give you good gallop.

2nd MAIDEN. I can be naked in one minute.

FORTINBRAS. Who taught you to say this?

1st MAIDEN. I love a good soldier.

2nd MAIDEN. Let's do it on the horse!

FORTINBRAS. My *palace guard* — ?! Do you even know what you're saying?

1st MAIDEN. *(Kneeling, kissing his hand chastely.)* Give it to me hot and heavy.

FORTINBRAS. Those — ! I'll have them *whipped! (The Maidens look anxious, confused.)* Not you! Listen — I need you for something honorable. I need you to marry me. *(They don't understand.)* To marry? Understand? *(He mimes putting a wedding ring on and off his finger. They confuse this with a graphic gesture.)*

MAIDENS. *(Shocked.) Oh — !*

FORTINBRAS. No — a *wife!* To take my mind off — I can't go into it right now. *(Grabbing the 2nd Maiden, placing her at his side, putting his arm through hers.)* Husband? Wife? Understand?

2nd MAIDEN. Have you ever seen such a big one?

FORTINBRAS. *Damn it!* It doesn't matter. I'm the King, and I can do what I want. I can even marry myself. Now — which one of you? Who cares, as long as you're not Ophelia. *(He clasps the 2nd Maiden a bit tighter. To the 1st Maiden.)* You can be the witness.

1st MAIDEN. Do you want me to watch?

FORTINBRAS. Right! *(To the 2nd Maiden.)* Do you, um ... before God and everybody, um ... take me for your lord and master and husband? Say "I do." *(She stares at him blankly.)* "I — do." Say it: "I — do."

2nd MAIDEN. *(Recognizing the phrase.)* Ah! I do it on the floor with you.

FORTINBRAS. No —

1st MAIDEN. I do it with everybody!

FORTINBRAS. No, not you! Don't answer.

2nd MAIDEN. I do whatever you say.

FORTINBRAS. Close enough! Good! And I, King Fortinbras of Denmark — and apparently several other places — take you for my wife, and promise to, um ... do a lot of things for you when I have time. All right? We're married.

1st MAIDEN. I will tickle you all night.

FORTINBRAS. No, no — you're not my wife. She is. I'm making a few changes, ok? One wife at a time. It's not you — you're lovely. It's just these damned ghosts.

HAMLET. *(Appearing behind them, carrying a book.)* We're not damned. We're not anything. *(They turn. All three see Hamlet.)*

FORTINBRAS. What do you want?!

HAMLET. Nothing. Just ... catching up on a little reading. *(The Maidens find Hamlet very impressive.)*

MAIDENS. Ooo!

FORTINBRAS. Hey — how come they can see you?

HAMLET. It seems to be getting harder for us to turn it on and off.

54

FORTINBRAS. *(As the Maidens gravitate unavoidably to Hamlet.)* Well, try!

HAMLET. I'm trying. *(This only impresses them more.)*

MAIDENS. *Ooooo!*

FORTINBRAS. I'm *married* to one of them!

HAMLET. Really? Which one?

FORTINBRAS. Um ... her.

HAMLET. What's her name?

FORTINBRAS. It doesn't matter! Keep your hands off! *(Moving the Maidens away.)* What is it with you ghosts? Do you have a special musk, or what?

HAMLET. *(To the Maidens, in Polish.)* I wish you both could stay.

MAIDENS. *Ooooh!!!*

FORTINBRAS. Stop it! Stop it! Don't tell me you speak Polish — !

HAMLET. I picked up a little at Wittenberg. *(To the Maidens, in Polish.)* Would you like to take a stroll?

1st MAIDEN. *(In Polish.)* I'd love to!

2nd MAIDEN. *(In Polish.)* Me too! *(Hamlet starts to escort them out.)*

FORTINBRAS. *(Pulling them back, away from him.)* Stop it! Get back here! Now! Right now!

MAIDENS. *(Disappointedly.)* Oooo...!

FORTINBRAS. Why don't you wait for me in the King's chambers? I'll be right there. *(The Maidens look blank.)* The King's chambers. The bedroom — where I go to sleep? *(Making a sleeping gesture.)* Sleep? Sleep? To sleep, perchance to — *(Fortinbras stops. A cold shiver goes through him. The Maidens stare at him concernedly.)* Get out! Get out! Go on! *(Frightened by his tone, the Maidens rush off.)* What's happening to me?

HAMLET. Could be a lot of things. The northerly climate, the disorder of the world, the elusiveness of your opponent.

FORTINBRAS. Which is?

HAMLET. Which is death.

FORTINBRAS. Polonius said I was in love with death.

HAMLET. He's entitled to his opinion. I never found him that well-read, myself. You seem awfully tense.

FORTINBRAS. Well, why not? I finally get my kingdom, and I can't even rule it, it's so plagued with ghosts.

HAMLET. I suspect it's pretty much like any kingdom — only here, we're more visible. When I was locked up in that box, I saw countless ghosts. All around me. Speaking innumerable languages. Dressed in fashions I'd never seen. Crowds of them. Multitudes.

FORTINBRAS. What is wrong with my army?

HAMLET. I'd only be guessing. I was never that much of a soldier. I spent most of my time at court, wondering what was wrong here. Maybe if you told my story.

FORTINBRAS. That story Horatio told me? With all the ridiculous — ?

HAMLET. It's true.

FORTINBRAS. It is? Even about the pirates? *(Hamlet nods.)* It doesn't matter. It's not what the people want to hear.

HAMLET. How do you know, unless you try?

FORTINBRAS. What do you care, anyway? You're dead.

HAMLET. If you pass through a desert, wandering, lost, you might leave a little cairn of stones. No one will ever find it. You yourself will die miles away, your body will disappear. Even the cairn will be buried, in time, by the sand. But somehow you want it to be there, the little mark, deep in the enormous heart of that wasteland. It may never be found, but it exists. Because you existed. That is how the truth works. *(Offering Fortinbras the book, which has no title on the cover.)* Hey, this is good — you want to read it?

FORTINBRAS. Not at the moment.

HAMLET. Well ... keep it anyway. Never know when the mood will strike. *(Hamlet hands Fortinbras the book. Fortinbras doesn't open it. Hamlet exits. Fortinbras looks at the book, opens it. He casually flips through a few pages, then something catches his eye. He starts reading more closely. He exits as he reads. Lights fade to black.)*

Scene 6

The courtyard. We see a man's legs dangling lifelessly at least ten feet above the ground. No more than the legs are visible. Horatio strides across the courtyard hurriedly. He doesn't see the legs. Horatio calls out loudly.

HORATIO.   Captain! Come here! *(The Captain appears.)* I've sent the King's message to our forces in the field. Tell me, has Osric been released?
CAPTAIN.   Released?
HORATIO.   Yes, released!
CAPTAIN.   From his suffering, you mean?
HORATIO.   Exactly.
CAPTAIN.   Oh. Absolutely. He's been released, all right. *(The Captain exits with a sidelong look at the legs. Horatio doesn't catch this. Instead, he breathes a great sigh of relief. He bends at the waist, letting his arms dangle. He straightens up, continuing this relaxing regimen into a stretch of his arms high above his head — at which point he sees the legs for the first time. He falls to the ground, shocked.)*
HORATIO.   My God! Osric! How could he?! How — !? You were innocent!! *You were innocent! (Osric enters from upstage.)*
OSRIC.   Relax. It wasn't anyone's fault. The Captain misunderstood.
HORATIO.   Osric! But ... aren't you...!?
OSRIC.   Yes. Very. "Release Osric from his suffering." That's how he put it. A rhetorical disaster.
HORATIO.   Then ... you're a — ?
OSRIC.   What else is new? There's more of us than you by now. You can't float down a corridor without bumping into two or three of us.
HORATIO.   How does it ... how does it feel?
OSRIC.   Oh, don't be a tourist. You'll find out soon enough. We all do.
HORATIO.   Can't you tell me anything?
OSRIC.   Only this: whatever you're doing to prepare for it,

don't bother.

HORATIO.   Why have you come back?

OSRIC.   Come back? I never left. Look at me — I was just hanged. *(They stare up at the lifeless legs.)* Don't know where I'm supposed to go. Just the same old faces, the same old walls. The only thing different is the way I feel.

HORATIO.   What do you mean?

OSRIC.   Suddenly I don't feel like pleasing everyone. I used to get so much satisfaction out of being of service. Now, I ... rather resent things.

HORATIO.   You have reason.

OSRIC.   Oh, drop that eternally earnest tone, will you?! *(Catching himself.)* There — you see? Resentment. Criticism. I don't know what's wrong with me. I should be looking for somebody to toady up to. Instead, I'm being ... abrasive.

HORATIO.   I'm sure it's in the service of some higher end.

OSRIC.   I don't think so. To be honest, I feel sort of ... on my own. *(Looking up at the legs again.)* It's not how I thought it would be. Then again, I'm not sure I ever thought of how it would be. Maybe it's different for everyone. Millions of different deaths. Just as there are millions of different lives. *(Turning suddenly to Horatio.)* Did that sound philosophical?

HORATIO.   A little.

OSRIC.   I've never been philosophical. *(Osric looks at the legs once more, then exits thoughtfully. Horatio stares after him. Suddenly Horatio draws his dagger and rushes out a different way.)*

HORATIO.   Fortinbras! Fortinbras!! *(Lights fade.)*

Scene 7

The King's chamber. The two Maidens are sitting in Fortinbras's bed, much as in Act One, Scene 4. Fortinbras enters, reading the book. He's startled to see the Maidens.

FORTINBRAS.   Oh! Yes ... you're here. The consummation! I completely forgot. *(The Maidens watch him a bit warily. The 1st*

Maiden puts her arm in front of the 2nd Maiden protectively.)

1st MAIDEN.   Bring on the regiment!

FORTINBRAS.   No, no — let's not talk. Shh, please? It's better if you don't ... talk. In fact ... *(Delicately taking the 1st Maiden by the hand and guiding her from the bed.)* It's better if you aren't in the bed at all.

1st MAIDEN.   *(Disappointedly.)* Oooo....

FORTINBRAS.   *(To the 1st Maiden.)* I'm afraid you'll have to wait out in the hall. *(The Maidens look at each other, worried about being separated.)*

1st MAIDEN.   *(Anxiously.)* Oooo...!

FORTINBRAS.   It's just for the night —

2nd MAIDEN.   Ooooo...!

FORTINBRAS.   *(To 2nd Maiden.)* Now, don't you start — !

MAIDENS.   *Ooooooo...!!!* *(The 1st Maiden slips out of his grasp and hurries back to the bed. Fortinbras sighs.)*

FORTINBRAS.   Ok. Ok. Why should anything be easy? *(Escorting the 1st Maiden out of the bed once more and towards a place to sit.)* You sit here. All right? And look the other way. Just ... the other way. *(As she does so.)* Good. Good enough. So, um ... wife — having exchanged our vows, pretty much — it's time that we ... um ... *(He sighs hopelessly, gets on the bed. He stares at her a moment, then raises the book that's still in his hand.)* Do you mind if I read a book? I know it may seem like an odd request, but actually I've gotten kind of ... involved ... *(He becomes engrossed in the book. She looks along with him.)* I feel so many things when I read it. Sensations. It's like I'm on the battlefield again. I can almost hear the sounds. You know, the way the men sound ... when they die. I wonder if this is what Horatio meant by an education. *(With a quick look to her.)* It's not about my battles — don't misunderstand. *(Thoughtfully.)* It's not really about me at all. *(The 2nd Maiden gently places her hand on his, stops him turning the pages. He stares at her. She hugs him comfortingly. At first he can't respond. Then he suddenly takes her in his arms and holds her tightly — almost desperately. Claudius and Gertrude enter. They rush to the bed. The Maidens can see them just fine.)*

CLAUDIUS.   It's true!

FORTINBRAS. What — ?!

GERTRUDE. Ophelia said you were getting married.

FORTINBRAS. What are you doing here?!

GERTRUDE. We've come to bless your union.

CLAUDIUS. Is this the consummation? We didn't want to be late. *(To Gertrude, of the bride.)* Isn't she lovely as a bride?

FORTINBRAS. Please — *go!*

CLAUDIUS. *(To the 1st Maiden.)* You're lovely, too. I hope I won't feel lust.

GERTRUDE. Don't speak of lust.

CLAUDIUS. How can I avoid it?

GERTRUDE. Think of the remorse!

FORTINBRAS. Get out of here! *Now!*

CLAUDIUS. We can't.

GERTRUDE. We're still in sacred ground.

CLAUDIUS. Please, unbury us. Hurry!

FORTINBRAS. Have you no sense of decorum? This is is my wedding night.

CLAUDIUS. We're heartily sorry, but we have no choice.

GERTRUDE. You must do it now — or you'll run out of time!

FORTINBRAS. *(Struck by her comment.)* What?!

CLAUDIUS. ... In your busy day.

FORTINBRAS. What's going on here?

GERTRUDE. Nothing.

CLAUDIUS. A minor disinterment — that's all we ask.

FORTINBRAS. *No!* Leave us! *(Claudius and Gertrude look at each other, then suddenly make a gesture. Instantly, the two Maidens can't see them. The Maidens look confused, fearful.)*

MAIDENS. Ooooooo...??! *(Gertrude and Claudius make another gesture.)*

CLAUDIUS. Hello again. *(The Maidens see them again.)*

MAIDENS. *Oooooooooo....!!!* *(The Maidens run from the room.)*

FORTINBRAS. I don't care how many maidens you scare away. I *won't* dig you up — understand?!

CLAUDIUS. Please.

GERTRUDE. Oh, please.

CLAUDIUS. *Please.*

FORTINBRAS.   Get out! *Get out, get out, get out, get out!!* (*Fortinbras closes his eyes as he pleads. During his speech, Hamlet, Ophelia, Polonius and Laertes enter to join the others around the bed.*) Just *go!* All of you — every ghost! I can't fight you anymore! What do you want from me? I know I didn't tell the truth, but who ever does?! Why won't you *depart!?* Why won't you let me be ... alive?! (*Fortinbras opens his eyes, sees them all.*)
LAERTES.   We can't go.
POLONIUS.   We need to be near you.
HAMLET.   At least, in spirit.
FORTINBRAS.   Ophelia — please! Get them to leave!
OPHELIA.   Oh — now you want a favor? Tell me, how's the consummation going?
FORTINBRAS.   Slow. Please, Ophelia. I'll do anything. I'm sorry I wanted to get married. I just thought you and Hamlet would be so much better suited —
OPHELIA.   I admit, he had me charmed for awhile. There's something about all that negativity. But I'm over it now. And I'm willing to forgive you. *If* you swear never to tell Hamlet's story.
CLAUDIUS.   He'll tell it.
LAERTES.   He must.
HAMLET.   All will come out.
OPHELIA.   (*To the ghosts.*) No, it won't! Why should it? Do you want to be remembered as a bunch of murderers, lechers, liars and fools?
POLONIUS.   If we must.
GERTRUDE.   It's our choice.
OPHELIA.   *It's not mine!* You were worse than me — all of you!
HAMLET.   We admit that.
OPHELIA.   Not enough! (*Quietly.*) Never enough.
CLAUDIUS.   It's over now.
GERTRUDE.   The time's up.
OPHELIA.   There's always time!
POLONIUS.   Not anymore.
FORTINBRAS.   What are you talking about?
POLONIUS.   Rest well, Fortinbras.

GERTRUDE.   Rest well.

HAMLET.   Rest, my friend.

LAERTES.   Rest. *(The other ghosts all look at Ophelia expectantly. She fights having to join this chorus, but something inside her is defeated, and she does so through clenched teeth.)*

OPHELIA.   *Rest, damn it!* (All the ghosts make the gesture Claudius and Gertrude made earlier in the scene. Now Fortinbras can't see them. He searches frantically as they all exit. He has the book.)*

FORTINBRAS.   Where are you? Where *are* you!? What's going on? *What's going on!?* (Horatio rushes in, his dagger ready.)* Horatio?!

HORATIO.   You villain! Osric is hanged!

FORTINBRAS.   Hanged? That's ridiculous — I freed him.

HORATIO.   He's hanging in the courtyard. Look for yourself! *(Fortinbras peers out a window. His eyes widen.)*

FORTINBRAS.   It's a mistake. My Captain must've —

HORATIO.   You killed him!

FORTINBRAS.   I didn't mean to —

HORATIO.   Prepare to die!

FORTINBRAS.   To die!? What are you — !

HORATIO.   *Someone, somewhere* is going to die for what they've done! Efficiently! At the appropriate time!

FORTINBRAS.   Just because I killed Osric? By mistake?

HORATIO.   Because someone's dead, and you're responsible. If my lord Hamlet had done what I'm about to do — *(He thrusts the dagger at Fortinbras, who dodges and tumbles over the bed.)*

FORTINBRAS.   *Horatio — !*

HORATIO.   Take death like a man!

FORTINBRAS.   *You* take death like a man! *(Horatio thrusts again, misses.)* Horatio ... Horatio — ! I'll tell the truth! Hamlet's true story!! I was going to do it anyway! I'll tell the truth!!

HORATIO.   *I'm sick of the truth!!* You know how many people I've tried to tell that story? You know how far I get?! Right up to the part where Hamlet walked *directly past Claudius* at prayer and didn't kill him! *(Missing again.)* I try to explain the religious underpinnings of his decision, the whole problem of

letting Claudius die shriven of his sins —
FORTINBRAS.   Of course —
HORATIO.   You think anyone believes me!? (*Fortinbras knocks the dagger from Horatio's hand and bolts. Horatio grabs him and pulls him back. Both men simultaneously reach for the foils on the wall. They fight briefly, Horatio nearly running Fortinbras through at one point.*)
FORTINBRAS.   Careful — ! (*Fortinbras trips and his foil goes flying. He scrabbles to his feet and Horatio stalks him.*) Horatio —
HORATIO.   "Would've killed him," they say! "The Hamlet we knew would've killed Claudius then and there! *Any* man would!!" (*Fortinbras makes a move for his sword, but Horatio grabs him and pushes him back on the bed, sword at his breast.*) You see?! They understand Elsinore better than we do! They know that here there's only one chance — one *split-second* — to take revenge! *If that!!*
FORTINBRAS.   Someone save me!! Ophelia! *OPHELIA!!!* (*Horatio pulls back to strike the death blow.*) NO!!!! (*Swift blackout.*)

Scene 8

The battlements. Fortinbras stands looking through a telescope. Arrayed behind him are Osric, Claudius and Gertrude with the same pile of regal objects. Ophelia and Laertes stand over to one side, Hamlet to the other. Polonius stands next to Fortinbras.

OSRIC.   (*As Gertrude and Claudius raise up the tapestry from the pile.*) What about this, Fortinbras?
FORTINBRAS.   Throw it in the moat.
GERTRUDE.   In the moat?
CLAUDIUS.   Are you sure?
FORTINBRAS.   *In the moat.* (*Looking through the telescope again, as the arras is thrown into the moat.*) Where's the army? They should be back by now.
POLONIUS.   It's a long and uncertain road. You've learned

that.

OPHELIA. *(Exasperatedly, to Polonius.)* Oh, please.

OSRIC. *(Holding up the chalice.)* Chalice?

FORTINBRAS. Moat.

OSRIC. Prayer bench?

FORTINBRAS. Moat.

CLAUDIUS. Moat?

OPHELIA. *(As these are thrown in.)* Why not toss it all in the moat?

FORTINBRAS. I intend to.

OPHELIA. And just how do you plan to revenge yourself on the living, if you leave them no reminders?

FORTINBRAS. I don't.

OPHELIA. But you were murdered.

FORTINBRAS. Not everything can work out. Oh, and thanks, everyone, for that great warning about my imminent death.

LAERTES. We gave you hints.

FORTINBRAS. Hints? "Rest well, Fortinbras"? It was bedtime! *(Looking through his telescope again.)* Why don't I know where my army is?! *(Horatio enters with a parchment.)*

HORATIO. I know where it is.

FORTINBRAS. You do? Excellent. Where?

HORATIO. *(Unrolling the parchment, reading.)* "A Summary of the Latest Events. The combined Danish-Norwegian-Polish-Carpathian-Transylvanian-Anatolian-Trans Caucasian-Persian-Afghan and Baluchistani forces under the supreme command of Fortinbras have reached the banks of the Indus River."

FORTINBRAS. So that's where they are.

HORATIO. "There they stood for a long time, staring across into that profound and endless universe of mysteries known as India."

FORTINBRAS. I distinctly told them to turn around.

HORATIO. "Poised for the final, inevitable conquest this proud array of forces, such as the world has never seen — the army of Fortinbras — "

OPHELIA. Get to the point.

HORATIO. "Laid down their arms — "

FORTINBRAS.   And started home?

HORATIO.   "And walked into the roiling Indus River, and drowned."

FORTINBRAS.   Drowned?

HORATIO.   To a man.

FORTINBRAS.   To a man? *(Horatio nods, reads on.)*

HORATIO.   There's one more item. "Horatio, having failed one prince and murdered another, today took his own life, in the Roman fashion. He can now — at last — be counted in the ranks of the dead. A distinction he holds in common with practically everyone he knew. Certainly everyone he cared about." *(Horatio looks first at Hamlet, then at Fortinbras, then reads on.)* "No one can fully explain the recent spate of untimely death within the walls of Elsinore — a seat of power and enlightenment once widely envied. Some have put forth the theory that death somehow became the fashion at court for a short time. Others think that a spiral of revenge more vicious and personal than ever before seen reigned here briefly. Still others think that the dead, having discovered that there is no final judgment, and sensing that they would soon dissipate into nothingness, forever — occupied themselves with the torture of the living. This manner of amusement sufficed only until so many had died that there was, in fact, no one worth taking revenge on any longer." *(Horatio rolls up the parchment, hands it to Osric.)* For the moat. *(Gently taking the telescope from Fortinbras.)* This too. *(Looking out over the battlement.)* When I first rode toward Elsinore, I thought, "What magnificence. How bright the future must be, if men have progressed so far as to build this." *(Horatio exits.)*

FORTINBRAS.   *(To Polonius.)* Was Horatio right about the army? *(Polonius starts to answer, decides against it, touches Fortinbras gently on the cheek, exits. To Hamlet.)* Was he? *(Ophelia moves to Fortinbras.)*

OPHELIA.   Why should you care? You're dead.

FORTINBRAS.   I was responsible. My whole army.

OPHELIA.   Oh, lighten up. Just means they'll get back here that much faster. Place is really going to be crowded.

FORTINBRAS.   We're going to disappear forever.

OPHELIA. *Will you stop talking like that!!?* Maybe those of you who had lives will disappear, since you don't need afterlives. But ... people like me —

LAERTES. *(Moving to Ophelia.)* Come on, Sis.

OPHELIA. *People like me ... ! (She can't finish.)*

LAERTES. Let's take a walk.

OPHELIA. With you? You can't even believe you're dead yet.

LAERTES. It's sinking in. *(Laertes escorts her out. Gertrude picks up the bouquet of dead flowers and drops them into the moat. She and Claudius exit as well.)*

FORTINBRAS. I'm sorry I killed you, Osric.

OSRIC. You ought to be. It was a dreadful mistake.

FORTINBRAS. Can you forgive me?

OSRIC. *(Making the bold choice.)* No. *(Osric smiles, pleased with himself, and exits. Fortinbras and Hamlet are alone. Hamlet bends down and picks up the only remaining object: the book.)*

HAMLET. For the moat? *(A beat. Hamlet moves towards the moat.)*

FORTINBRAS. No! Um ...

HAMLET. Yes?

FORTINBRAS. I ... can't decide.

HAMLET. Well, when you read it, how did you like it?

FORTINBRAS. I was ... captivated. Is that the right word?

HAMLET. Yes. *(With a look around.)* They'll tell a story about this place, no matter what we do. It could still be this one. *(Fortinbras hesitates, then reaches for the book. Hamlet hands it to him. Fortinbras holds it a moment, takes in the view one last time, then sets the book down on the battlement. The two men exit together, smiling. After a moment, Marcellus and Barnardo enter quickly — each of them arm in arm with one of the Maidens. They stare out over the battlement.)*

MARCELLUS. *(Pointing.)* There! There's where we saw it!

1st MAIDEN. *(Not understanding, but catching his mood.)* Ooooo!

BARNARDO. The ghost of Hamlet's father!

2nd MAIDEN. Ooooo.

MARCELLUS. *(Picking up the book.)* What's this?

BARNARDO. I don't know. *(Barnardo prepares to throw it over the battlement. The Maidens quickly reach for it.)*

MAIDENS. *Ooooooo — !*

BARNARDO. You want it? *(The Maidens nod. The 2nd Maiden opens the book, turns to a page at random. She starts to sound out the words with her usual strong accent.)*

2nd MAIDEN. "For in ... For in dat —

MARCELLUS. *(Looking over her shoulder.)* That.

2nd MAIDEN. "That ... Sleep? Sleep of ... "

BARNARDO. Death.

2nd MAIDEN. "Death. For in that sleep of death, what ... um — "

MARCELLUS. Dreams may come.

2nd MAIDEN. "Dreams".

1st MAIDEN. *(Also starting to read.)* "Venn ve haf ... haf —"

BARNARDO. "When. When we have shuffled off — "

1st MAIDEN. *(Eager to continue by herself.)* "Shuffled off ... dis ... mortal ... um —"

2nd MAIDEN. "Mortal ... ?"

MARCELLUS. "Coil."

MAIDENS. *(Together, nodding and smiling with accomplishment.)* *Ah!* "Coil."

MARCELLUS. That's right — coil. *(The Maidens beam at their book. Barnardo looks uncertainly at Marcellus.)*

BARNARDO. Coil? *(Marcellus shrugs. The Maidens look at the book. The men too are drawn back to its pages. Lights fade to black.)*

THE END

PROPERTY LIST

Foils
Chalis
Pearl
Telescope (Fortinbras)
Tapestry (Marcellus, Barnardo)
Parchment (Horatio)
Pile of "regal objects"
Dried flower bouquet (Osric)
Small wooden prayer bench
Sealed parchment (Captain)
Cloth bag with melon (Captain)
Knife (Horatio)
Crown (Fortinbras)
Television
Torches (Marcellus; Barnardo)
Dagger (Laertes; Horatio)
TV remote control (Ophelia)
Book (Hamlet)
Dangling legs (one pair)

NEW PLAYS

• **MERE MORTALS by David Ives, author of *All in the Timing*.** Another critically acclaimed evening of one-act comedies combining wit, satire, hilarity and intellect -- a winning combination. The entire evening of plays can be performed by 3 men and 3 women. ISBN: 0-8222-1632-9

• **BALLAD OF YACHIYO by Philip Kan Gotanda.** A provocative play about innocence, passion and betrayal, set against the backdrop of a Hawaiian sugar plantation in the early 1900s. *"Gotanda's writing is superb ... a great deal of fine craftsmanship on display here, and much to enjoy."* --*Variety*. *"...one of the country's most consistently intriguing playwrights..."* --*San Francisco Examiner*. *"As he has in past plays, Gotanda defies expectations..."* --*Oakland Tribune*. [3M, 4W] ISBN: 0-8222-1547-0

• **MINUTES FROM THE BLUE ROUTE by Tom Donaghy.** While packing up a house, a family converges for a weekend of flaring tempers and shattered illusions. *"With MINUTES FROM THE BLUE ROUTE [Donaghy] succeeds not only in telling a story -- a typically American one with wide appeal, about how parents and kids struggle to understand each other and mostly fail -- but in notating it inventively, through wittily elliptical, crisscrossed speeches, and in making it carry a fairly vast amount of serious weight with surprising ease."* --*Village Voice*. [2M, 2W] ISBN: 0-8222-1608-6

• **SCAPIN by Molière, adapted by Bill Irwin and Mark O'Donnell.** This adaptation of Molière's 325-year-old farce, *Les Fourberies de Scapin*, keeps the play in period while adding a late Twentieth Century spin to the language and action. *"This SCAPIN, [with a] felicitous adaptation by Mark O'Donnell, would probably have gone over big with the same audience who first saw Molière's Fourberies de Scapin...in Paris in 1671."* --*N.Y. Times*. *"Commedia dell'arte and vaudeville have at least two things in common: baggy pants and Bill Irwin. All make for a natural fit in the celebrated clown's entirely unconventional adaptation."* --*Variety* [9M, 3W, flexible] ISBN: 0-8222-1603-5

• **THE TURN OF THE SCREW adapted for the stage by Jeffrey Hatcher from the story by Henry James.** The American master's classic tale of possession is given its most interesting "turn" yet: one woman plays the mansion's terrified governess while a single male actor plays everyone else. *"In his thoughtful adaptation of Henry James' spooky tale, Jeffrey Hatcher does away with the supernatural flummery, exchanging the story's balanced ambiguities about the nature of reality for a portrait of psychological vampirism..."* --*Boston Globe*. [1M, 1W] ISBN: 0-8222-1554-3

• **NEVILLE'S ISLAND by Tim Firth.** A middle management orientation exercise turns into an hilarious disaster when the team gets "shipwrecked" on an uninhabited island. *"NEVILLE'S ISLAND ... is that rare event: a genuinely good new play..., it's a comedic, adult LORD OF THE FLIES..."* --*The Guardian*. *"... A non-stop, whitewater deluge of comedy both sophisticated and slapstick.... Firth takes a perfect premise and shoots it to the extreme, flipping his fish out of water, watching them flop around a bit, and then masterminding the inevitable feeding frenzy."* --*New Mexican*. [4M] ISBN: 0-8222-1581-0

DRAMATISTS PLAY SERVICE, INC.
440 Park Avenue South, New York, NY 10016 212-683-8960 Fax 212-213-1539
postmaster@dramatists.com www.dramatists.com

NEW PLAYS

- **TAKING SIDES by Ronald Harwood.** Based on the true story of one of the world's greatest conductors whose wartime decision to remain in Germany brought him under the scrutiny of a U.S. Army determined to prove him a Nazi. *"A brave, wise and deeply moving play delineating the confrontation between culture, and power, between art and politics, between irresponsible freedom and responsible compromise."* --London Sunday Times. [4M, 3W] ISBN: 0-8222-1566-7

- **MISSING/KISSING by John Patrick Shanley.** Two biting short comedies, MISSING MARISA and KISSING CHRISTINE, by one of America's foremost dramatists and the Academy Award winning author of *Moonstruck. " ... Shanley has an unusual talent for situations ... and a sure gift for a kind of inner dialogue in which people talk their hearts as well as their minds...." --N.Y. Post.* MISSING MARISA [2M], KISSING CHRISTINE [1M, 2W] ISBN: 0-8222-1590-X

- **THE SISTERS ROSENSWEIG by Wendy Wasserstein, Pulitzer Prize-winning author of *The Heidi Chronicles.*** Winner of the 1993 Outer Critics Circle Award for Best Broadway Play. A captivating portrait of three disparate sisters reuniting after a lengthy separation on the eldest's 50th birthday. *"The laughter is all but continuous." --New Yorker. "Funny. Observant. A play with wit as well as acumen.... In dealing with social and cultural paradoxes, Ms. Wasserstein is, as always, the most astute of commentators." --N.Y. Times.* [4M, 4W] ISBN: 0-8222-1348-6

- **MASTER CLASS by Terrence McNally. Winner of the 1996 Tony Award for Best Play.** Only a year after winning the Tony Award for *Love! Valour! Compassion!,* Terrence McNally scores again with the most celebrated play of the year, an unforgettable portrait of Maria Callas, our century's greatest opera diva. *"One of the white-hot moments of contemporary theatre. A total triumph." --N.Y. Post. "Blazingly theatrical." -- USA Today.* [3M, 3W] ISBN: 0-8222-1521-7

- **DEALER'S CHOICE by Patrick Marber.** A weekly poker game pits a son addicted to gambling against his own father, who also has a problem but won't admit it. *"... make tracks to DEALER'S CHOICE, Patrick Marber's wonderfully masculine, razor-sharp dissection of poker-as-life.... It's a play that comes out swinging and never lets up -- a witty, wisecracking drama that relentlessly probes the tortured souls of its six very distinctive ... characters. CHOICE is a cutthroat pleasure that you won't want to miss." --Time Out (New York).* [6M] ISBN: 0-8222-1616-7

- **RIFF RAFF by Laurence Fishburne.** RIFF RAFF marks the playwriting debut of one of Hollywood's most exciting and versatile actors. *"Mr. Fishburne is surprisingly and effectively understated, with scalding bubbles of anxiety breaking through the surface of a numbed calm." --N.Y. Times. "Fishburne has a talent and a quality...[he] possesses one of the vital requirements of a playwright -- a good ear for the things people say and the way they say them." --N.Y. Post.* [3M] ISBN: 0-8222-1545-4

DRAMATISTS PLAY SERVICE, INC.
440 Park Avenue South, New York, NY 10016 212-683-8960 Fax 212-213-1539
postmaster@dramatists.com www.dramatists.com